Someone K*
Sending Me*
Flowers

Ferndale Community School L.R.C

BOOK:

AUTHOR:

Return by:
Return by:
Return by:
Return by:
Return by:
Return by:
Return by:
Return by:
Return by:
Return by:
Return by:
Return by:
Return by:
Return by:

*For Mary Joan
and Brian*

Someone Keeps Sending Me Flowers

More reflections
and prayers.

Graham English

Collins Dove
Melbourne Australia

COLLINS DOVE
60-64 Railway Road, Blackburn, Victoria 3130
Telephone (03) 877 1333

First published 1989

Cover illustration by Graham English
Designed by Judith Summerfeldt
Typeset in 12/13 Garamond by Typeset Gallery, Malaysia
Printed in Australia by The Book Printer

The National Library of Australia
Cataloguing-in-Publication Data

English, Graham.
    Someone keeps sending me flowers.

    ISBN 0 85924 772 4.

    I. Title.

A823'.3

Contents

Someone keeps sending me flowers

Someone has been sending me flowers. It has been going on now for years. Sometimes a bunch. Sometimes just one. Or two. Each time a note: 'I love you'. Waratahs, wattles, roses. 'I love you, Graham, I love you.'

Someone has been sending me love songs. It has been going on for years. Currawongs sing them and magpies. Lorrikeets yell them, cockatoos squeal them. 'I love you', they sing. 'I love you.' Sometimes they are accompanied by drums and guitars. Sometimes the piano. I'm in the mood for love. In the mood. In the mood. Someone is singing me love songs.

Someone is making me laugh. It has been going on for years. Michael Leunig, Woody Allen, Spike Milligan, Wendy Harmer, Debbie and Tim. 'We love', they say, and I laugh. It must be okay because we are laughing. I'll send them all some flowers, or sing them a song. I love laughing.

And sometimes I cry.

The flowers never last. I have seen people walking on roses and wondered why. Why crush beautiful things? I have seen grey days and wondered if any flower would ever bloom anywhere ever again.

Sometimes the message has been unclear. It seemed to stop coming. 'Does anyone love me?' I wondered. 'Who could love me? I'm all wrong. I'm no good at that and all the wrong shape and I won't pass and they'll all laugh harshly.'

Sometimes the song stops. All I hear are jarring noises, crashing and beating. Or silence. Nothing. Nothing.

Then I think of the flowers and the songs and I laugh. I can love. I am loveable. I am loved. I have felt warmed and hugged. I am here because I'm here because I'm here. Erin hugs me. Max hugs me. Mark hugs me. Dorothy hugs me. I exist. If I could I would walk on my hands.

Someone is sending me flowers. 'I love you.' Someone up there loves ME.

I am loveable.

Someone sent his son for me. 'I love you,' he said, 'I would die for you'. Like a waratah in the bush or a hillside of wattle. Flash. Startle. Who me? Love the tear, dry the face, watch the smile. Every time. After the storm the rainbow. After the flood the dove. After the death the rising. I am loveable. I am loved. Someone keeps sending me flowers.

I am locked up in myself. I cannot talk or scream. I am wrong. But someone keeps sending me waratahs. There's a hillside of wattle. The trees are full of currawongs. Sing, sing. The air is full of cockatoos. Fly, fly, fly. Someone up there, someone down here, someone, someone, someone loves ME.

I will send you flowers. I will sing you a song. I will laugh and laugh with you. Someone loves us. I love us. I love you because someone keeps sending me flowers. I love you. Very much. That's why I keep sending you flowers.

Creating God, thank you for me, for the flowers, the songs and the laughs. And thank you for the grey days. They help me see the flowers. Amen

Anzac Day

At St Mary's church they were never sure whether it was Anzac Day or not, because it is also the feast of St Mark. Was it red vestments for martyrs or black for our glorious dead? They compromised. At seven o'clock mass they had red. At nine o'clock black.

At nine o'clock mass there was a pretend coffin with a flag, a digger's hat and a bayonet. It stood for the dead. Their names were listed on the town hall and on monuments from Perth to Gisborne. Their ages were not listed but had they put nineteen beside them all they'd have made few mistakes.

Anzac Day is for all the war dead, but especially for Gallipoli. My mother had three cousins killed there. Maybe more. There is Paterson's Curse at Gallipoli, Riverina bluebell. It is recorded that some of the lads thought it was a lot like home there in the Dardenelles; they thought of coming back after the war and taking up land.

The cadets practised for weeks for the nine o'clock mass. The slide, slide of the slow march up the isle and the muffled order, 'Reverse arms', are my strongest Anzac memories. It was mystical standing there watching. Ross Hanns on the guard wearing the medals his father left after he'd died at Balikpapan. I thought of Miro Marketo. I found his name one day, pencilled inside my desk. The desks at our school were made when they broke up the ark. Miro had lived around the corner in Thornhill Lane. He'd been the champion footballer at school. Next year he was killed over Europe. Now Thornhill Lane is called Miro Street.

Some of the Anzac mass was melodrama, like the dipping of flags and the salute at the altar. Jesus is not my general. About that time I found an old belt buckle. 'Got mit uns', it read. I asked at school. 'God is with us.' Later there was a song. 'With God on our side'. O god of battles you are not my God.

And the sermon was usually mediocre. Always the quote about laying down your life for your friend, but always some ambiguity. What did the day really mean? Should we celebrate it at all? And what about the Protestants? They'd all met at dawn, with a few stray Catholics, and they had a service after at the picture theatre. We could not go. We had the mass.

At the march we clapped the Brothers' boys and the convent girls. We clapped, too, for the men we knew. Like old Scotty Loman, who'd got on the rum at the Somme and never got off. Usually he sat on the seat outside the railway station but today was his big day. We were less generous to the Scouts and the Red Cross girls. When the silence came we had been told to pray. I felt superior. I prayed for the Protestants. I did not pray for the Turks, the Germans or the Japanese. I do now.

We missed a war. We had been war babies. Our

mothers had been left at home like their mothers before them. Those just younger did not miss. I stood later in the cemetery in Canberra as they buried Baron Smith. There were pink blossoms in the trees and angry young men standing helpless around the grave.

This year the Anzac mass will be white. In Turkey it will be spring and the hills will be purple with Paterson's Curse. Turks call it *Yelkovon*. It is an archaic Turkish word and it means 'irresponsible'.

God of peace, God of hope, lead us on. Amen.

Come as you are

I was going to mass on a balmy April evening. Near the door of the church a man said, 'Hello there, brother'. Embarrassed by his warmth, I grinned, 'Hello there'. I couldn't manage the 'brother'. I walked in. The people were talking, welcoming, laughing. 'Would you say one of these prayers of the faithful?' a young woman asked me. 'Yes I'd like to', I said. She went about asking others. An old lady was kneeling in the Sacrament chapel saying her beads, head bowed.

Most of the ordinary people looked ordinary. Some looked very poor. Near me was an old lady with nearly no teeth. A young man, a school teacher, had his arm around her shoulder. 'How are you Wilma?' he said. 'Good thanks', she replied. I thought of the old lady with only two teeth, one at the top and one at the bottom—luckily they met. I laughed. No one here came out of *Vogue* magazine.

There was singing to begin. Good singing because all the people joined in. The church was dilapidated though it looked well used and cared for in a way. 'We use this place' seemed to sum it up. The acoustics were not good. The church had been designed for something different; for silence mostly.

The priest knew everyone by name and they knew him by name. He did not have a title. Some called him Father, but it was not a title. He was fatherly to them. Some called him Mike because it was his Christian name.

Women and men took part. Black and white, people who spoke Australian clearly, people who spoke it poorly. A derelict man walked in. 'Hello there, brother,' he was told, 'take a seat'.

We listened to the reading: 'There are no distinctions between Jew and Greek, slave and free, male and female, but all of you are one in Jesus Christ'. Nor poor nor rich, clean or dirty, reputable or disreputable, Caucasian or Asian, I thought. Fill in your own distinctions then say, 'There are no distinctions'.

A woman stood and spoke to us. 'Today's first collection is to bail out Cheeky Bunjil', she said. 'I need another sixty dollars.' As the plate passed me I saw a twenty dollar note and a ten and several fives. Father Mike spoke. 'Some of our people are demonstrating against war, against the preparation for war. They are not demonstrating against sin that is about to be committed, against sin that will be committed. They are demonstrating against sin that is being committed. To get ready for war is to make war.'

The sign of peace was a lively affair. The whole mass had been until then, with people wandering about, everyone taking part, joining in. But the sign of peace had special meaning. No one was less important. It was a come-as-you-are mass. It was a come-as-you-are sign of peace. God loves you as you are.

At communion Mike and George gave communion on our side; Heidi, a pregnant woman, and Evonne, a black woman, gave communion on the other side. 'I shall not call you servants anymore because a servant does not know the master's business: I shall call you friends.' There is no power here, there is only friendship in the Lord. Near me a tiny baby was being passed to an old lady who wanted to cuddle it. How radical Christ's message is if you take it seriously! Of course they executed him for it. No wonder. If you were accused of being Christlike could they find enough evidence? Would you get off on a technicality?

Iris Murdoch said, 'Writing is like getting married. One should never commit oneself until one is amazed at one's luck'. I think Christianity is like getting married. One should never commit oneself until one is amazed at one's luck.

Too often Christianity as it is experienced by us is not amazing. That's why so few people are committed. We are such dreadful witnesses.

God you are amazing. Help us to be amazed and help us to live as if we are. Amen.

Walk on your hands

The Bishop used to drink a bit. We all knew. But they didn't mention it in his obituary. Now I don't like drunks. I find it hard to laugh at drunks. But I'm surprised they neglected to mention it.

He did silly things when he'd been drinking—like walking on his hands. When he was young he could walk on his hands like I can walk on my feet. Better really, because I stoop. When he was drunk he felt young, and there he'd go on his hands. You could pick it on a Sunday. He'd be at an opening, giving his 'Right Reverend Monsignori speech', with an elastoplast on his forehead where he'd fallen, or gravel rash on his nose. The dark rings under his eyes did nothing to make him more cheerful looking.

I suppose he was lonely. Or maybe he felt wasted, out of due place or time. I used to think he'd have been better in Florence with Michelangelo. But they should have mentioned it in his obituary.

I can cope with a bishop who drinks a bit. I think I

could cope with a bishop who had a mistress. I can

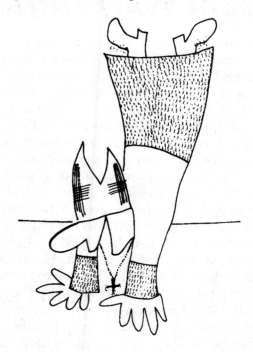

understand that. But I could not cope with a bishop who was scared. Not frightened. Anyone can get frightened. But scared!

Of course there is a precedent for a bishop being scared. Peter the apostle was scared. But that was before Pentecost. Afterwards he was still a conservative pushed around by conservatives. Paul had an awful fight with him about whether gentile men had to be circumcised if they became Christians. I am glad Paul won. I am also glad that someone recorded the fight because it reminds me that it's all right for the main bishop, in this case Peter, to be wrong. The Holy Spirit didn't promise that being a bishop meant you wouldn't have to say you're sorry.

But Peter was not scared after Pentecost. He was a

courageous conservative. And Paul was not scared. He was a courageous radical and a hard man to live with I think.

I'd have trouble with a scared bishop as I have trouble with any scared leader. Scared leaders are penny wise and pound foolish. They are scared to make a mistake. A painter friend pointed out to me that art conceals art. An artist makes art look easy. Like Picasso. If you think a child could draw a Picasso, you have a go. Like a Bobby Simpson slips catch. He made it look simple. All the hard work was hidden. Like a Joan Sutherland aria. The practice is not evident. If you can see the effort the person may be a good trier. If you can see the effort the person is not an artist.

In a way the drinking bishop was an artist. A flawed artist, like every artist. At the things he was good at he was very good. And he wasn't scared. He made some whopping mistakes because he didn't know when to give up walking on his hands. That's why they should have mentioned it in his obituary.

Art can be sought and worked for but in the end it is a gift. I cannot be Bobby Simpson no matter how I try. But not being scared would be a start. The bishop was not scared. Drunk yes, but not scared.

God most high, help us so that we are not scared. Send your Spirit to make us courageous. Amen.

McGilligutty's sister

McGilligutty's sister could climb to the top of telegraph posts and she could swing by her legs on the horizontal bar in the Brothers' yard. The Sisters on the verandah of the convent over beyond the corrugated iron fence looked on. Some tut-tutted and spoke to her on Monday morning. Others envied her, dressed as they were in top to heels clothes that suited a northern winter in the thirteenth century.

McGilligutty's sister went everywhere with McGilligutty and his brother. She was the one who was always sent to get permission. 'I won't ask unless you let me come', she'd say. Together they explored the whole place, forbidden territories and all. 'Keep away from the creek' they'd be warned. 'Yes', they'd chorus, but like the good moralists they were being trained to be at St Mary's, they'd make a mental reservation. 'Yes', they'd say aloud. 'When we're twenty one', they'd say in their heads. The catechism was by no means always a thing to hold people in. The catechism was a two-edged sword.

Once their moral gymnastics had come undone! There were large boxthorn bushes down the creek. They referred to them as the briars. Generations of youthful explorers had tunnelled under them playing bushrangers or pirates or something else. The McGilligutty's were exploring, carrying lighted candles, not that it was very dark but to lend atmosphere. McGilligutty's sister, ahead of him, tried out her candle on a protruding thorn and kept going, leaving it red hot. Well, McGilligutty didn't notice and, as he passed, the red hot briar touched the back of his neck!

The nearest funnel web spider was a hundred miles away in fact, but on McGilligutty's neck in imagination. 'Oh my God, I am very sorry,' he screamed in a desperate attempt to avoid a sudden and unprovided death. The uncontrolled laughter of his siblings signalled that his devout act of contrition was premature even if innately worth while. 'Now look what you've made me go and do', he said, trying to regain some dignity. He'd probably have hit one or the other but for the knowledge that in either case he'd have come second.

McGilligutty's sister had talents different from her brothers'. She was less easily cowed for a start. This was not quickly appreciated nor understood. The result was that she suffered for not being someone else, a not uncommon suffering for the younger members of some families. Not being easily cowed was a disadvantage too. That is a gift some younger siblings are given but it brings its heartaches as well. Maybe questioning is a special female gift, though not all have it, and my closest female friend, a great questioner, isn't sure about female gifts, or male gifts. Just human gifts. Still, questioning is a great gift though not always valued. Or at least that's McGilligutty's experience.

Give us questioners Lord, and people not easily cowed. And thank you for McGilligutty's sister. Amen.

Captain Catholic

Captain Catholic flew down and landed on the sand. 'Not even a footprint,' he thought. 'Deft eh?' He strode to the nearby change shed and changed. Eagle-eye HogShed always knew he was special. The others struggled with the catechism. Not he. By the age of eleven he knew it backwards. 'Dlrow eht edam dog', he'd snap back if you asked him who made the world. 'Eb ti yam os snaem nema', he'd shout if you asked him what 'Amen' meant. People looked on amazed.

When at the age of fifteen Eagle-eye found one day that he could fly, he was not surprised. He knew there was something special about him. He had his mother make him a suit with a cloak, blue and white because it seemed mystical, and besides, he could wear it to the football. He called himself Captain Catholic and determined to set things right.

HogShed saw that there were two enemies. There was the enemy Without and the enemy Within. Without and Within were twins, though not identical. Of the two he thought Within the worse.

As Captain Catholic, HogShed had special vision. He could see around corners. This gave him the ability to see logical outcomes. It also had one disability. Seeing around corners makes it difficult to distinguish between objects and so Captain could not tell the difference between Within and Without. However, as he knew they were enemies he devised a simple plan. 'If in doubt, STRIKE' he'd had embroidered on his belt.

IT LOOKS LIKE A JOB FOR CAPTAIN CATHOLIC...

HogShed *knew* his catechism backwards. He was less sure of his Bible. He knew his enemies though, and so a vaguely remembered gospel quote came to him: 'He who is not me is against me'. That sounded right, he thought. He delved into philosophy as well. 'I am therefore I am right', suited him fine. The fact that he could fly and see around corners gave Captain Catholic great confidence in himself. He began to contemplate his enemies.

The enemy Without was evil and took many forms. But Within was myriad and far, far worse. Within, in whatever form, had this gravest of faults, the inability to see that HogShed was always right.

HogShed *knew* that what he felt or believed or had been taught by Sister Matilda was self-evidently true. So it followed that anyone who disagreed with him was obviously in bad faith and was therefore the enemy Within. Now wrong has no rights. Father Nono had taught him that. So HogShed had no compunction when it came to the enemy Within. Destruction was HogShed's hobby and the enemy Within was his target.

Within's sin was lack of will. HogShed had no such lack. Within used words like imagine, free, choose, peace, life. HogShed reminded all of death. 'Do not think, or ask,' said HogShed, 'lest you disagree with me'. Worse than thinking, Within sometimes doubted. You can see why Eagle-eye was upset! 'Imagine promoting reading', he shuddered. 'Ban bad books. Burn them. Maybe we could burn Within.' He rubbed his hands at the thought. 'After all, if Within's going to burn, we might as well begin it.'

Captain Catholic marched up and down. He planned and connived all in the name of the truth, his truth. Enemies beware, Without and Within. He wrote letters, rang up, made contacts. Right, right, right, right, right. 'Keep in step there', he said.

I Am Who I Am, help me to think. Reassure me that it is all right to be unsure. I am content to leave footsteps in the sand. Your son, Amen.

Thou mothering me God

Punt was a Protestant who did not like statues. 'Idolatory', he'd been heard to whisper when they were mentioned. So when he became enthusiastic about one, one morning sitting under the Tree of Knowledge on Major Briggs' Corner, Woodbridge and Galpin were surprised.

Woodbridge was a Catholic who loved statues, though usually not the ones he'd grown up with, even the new wooden versions that had become popular since Vatican II. Galpin was somewhere in between, church and statue-wise.

'I was in the grounds of St Patrick's', began Punt. 'I was there visiting my Aunt Adelaide. And I was feeling a bit down. Funny how thoughts just slip into your head. I thought—I wonder if God even knows I'm here?' Woodbridge and Galpin looked sympathetic and Galpin gave a Rogerian grunt. 'Then I saw this statue, a great marble thing with 'Pray for Brigid and Timothy Prendergast' on a brass plate on its side.' He paused and looked a bit uncomfortable. 'Well I walked around to the front. It was a statue of Jesus and he was pointing to his heart. And suddenly I felt warm. He does know, I thought. His heart is the sign. I always thought it was stupid and suddenly that heart thing made sense to me. I've always been a thinking man but here I *felt* something. Jesus feels for me. What do you think of that?'

Galpin looked perplexed. 'I don't know', he said. 'I have trouble with bits of bodies. Sacred hearts and precious blood and all that. It's all a bit like the Red Cross to me. Don't you think so Woodbridge?'

Woodbridge was gazing down the street, idly picking peppercorns from the tree above him and throwing them at a pot-hole in the road. He was missing the hole mostly. 'I used to. I thought it mawkish. But I've changed. Heart of God, sure. But I think more of the womb of God. Thou mothering me God, to misquote the poet. Thou mothering me. I'd like to have a feast of the Womb of God. I think that God is mother to the world and to all people. God is grunting in birth. Maybe we should have a statue.'

Galpin groaned. 'No statue', he said. 'Maybe a painting though. I read once that we're supposed to be mothers of God, giving birth to Christ in the world. It has possibilities this line of thinking.'

Punt was not sure. 'What have I started?' he asked.

'Oh you didn't start it really. The idea of the motherhood of God has been around for a long time. It's just some of the implications that I've started thinking of—God being feminine, God's breasts nourishing humanity, God keening for the deaths that we die and cause, God encouraging and cherishing us. Calling someone a real old woman would be calling someone God-like.'

'I think', said Galpin, 'I was wrong. A statue—granite, like Henry Moore.' 'Or bronze, like Degas', said Punt.

20

'Rouault could have painted the mothering God.'

Thou mothering me, God. Amen.

Harvest festival

Christ is the seed and Christ is the harvest.

Easter has no meaning for those who have not faced their own death, at least a little. It is all very well to say that unless the grain of wheat dies there is no plant and no harvest. It is living it that is the hard part.

Cardinal Paul Arns was asked how he kept on in spite of the risks. His answer was that if you are not afraid of death there is not a lot they can do to you. Of course Cardinal Arns has the advantage of being celibate. He has no spouse or children to consider. But it is a good point. Again, though, it is easier said than done.

Paul Ricoeur says that the process of becoming conscious is ultimately a process of seeing one's childhood in front of oneself and one's death behind oneself.

To put death behind, to be unafraid of death, to be able to live Christ's claim that it is necessary to die before the harvest: how do I begin?

Maybe we could begin by looking at our experience of death.

There are the experiences of others' deaths, when people leave us who we desperately wanted to stay. But the death I am talking about is the death that takes place in us. Think of your own death experiences; the 'I could have died' times, the 'a part of me died' experiences, the times you knew in your heart or your stomach that you are mortal.

I am bad at sport. I grew up in a place where ability at football was very important. I was the one they picked last. I was the one they fought not to have in their team. My father has Alzheimer's disease. His memory has gone. When, finally, I was adult enough to need to talk to him as an adult he was gone. That is a dying experience. Some of my dying experiences, the ones that still cause me grief, some that I still struggle against though the struggle nought availeth, are too close to talk of here.

What are your dying experiences? You will know because we all do, right from our earliest days when we cannot have our own way, when even the fulfilment of our desires does not satisfy us for long. We all know, or we will somewhere along the line, that when all is said and done there is nowhere to run.

Then there is Easter! Having died we will be raised. What are your life experiences? Because Easter is the celebration of God's promise to us that death will not have the victory. That's why Cardinal Arns and Paul Ricoeur know that we must look forward to our childhood, to our rebirth.

What are your life experiences? The times you knew life was worth while?

Once we were lucky enough to drive over the Pyrenees. Our old van struggled up and up at five miles an hour for what seemed a very long time. Our whole concern was, 'Will it get us there?' Then at the top, all unexpected and unasked for, a view beyond description. It was one of those 'If heaven is better than this it must be good' experiences. A friend told me of going off to have a baby and coming home and finding the peach tree broken out in blossom, a sign of welcome to the new child.

Take some time to think about your life experiences. These are the harvest experiences. Easter is about the fact that Christ faced my death with me, Christ became the seed for me. Then Christ was raised. I will be at the harvest. *Alleluia.*

Benediction

'All your lessons are about death or sex.' I'd just finished teaching poetry in Year Eleven.

'What else is there?' I laughed, only half joking. I thought she was probably wrong, so quickly examined my lessons. Of course I teach about other things.

I grew up surrounded by death and sex. Close to the earth. I was told nothing about sex. I was told a lot about death.

In kindergarten we played on the grave of the old priest, hiding behind the great Gaelic cross that marked his rest. Often as we went into the church there was a coffin there. Funerals were part of the life of a country town and especially of a country Catholic school. 'Someone's died', I remember saying as a tiny child—as an aeroplane went overhead. Somehow I had the idea it was taking a soul to heaven.

We knew people who died. My cousin Pat was thrown by a horse. I remember going to the fete with him one day. Next week he was dead. Later I knew boys who were killed out shooting, and a little pretty girl who died of polio. I remember being scared and praying that I'd be safe.

Aunts and uncles, brothers and sisters of my grandparents, and my grandparents, died one by one. There'd be the rosary down at Patterson the undertaker's. 'Aunty Rachel looked so peaceful', they'd say when they came back. 'Her hair was in a plait and she just looked asleep.' We'd meet all the relations—the McLarens and the Ritchies, the Campbells and the Boorowa Carmodys. When old Uncle Henry was dying we'd take blancmange up to the home to him. We knew he had cancer and couldn't eat anything else.

Sometimes you'd hear stories of wakes, but by then it was always. 'In the old days at Boorowa' or 'When Aunty Alice died at Frogmore'. We'd forgotten our Irish heritage. We were Australians and there was none of that. Death was entirely religious. And loss. But we were scared of death. The priests saw to that. There was this inconsistency. There were all these good people—really good people, and they were scared stiff of God, and we were scared too. God waited to get people. God was unfair and arbitrary, and because he gave us more he expected very much.

One night when I was very young, Mum and Father took us to Benediction. I was used to the church in daylight. The church at night was magic when I was seven. The stained glass was black, the altar glowed. There were candles and flowers, gladioli or dahlias. The priest and altar boys wore white and gold and red. High above, Jesus glowed in the monstrance. Latin hymns and incense made that black behind the altar seem like a magic cave.

That's why I stayed.

Now I am not scared of God. Except when I am depressed and my childhood God beats at my head or heart. That God was a trick to try to make me stay.

Poor miserable God. God the debt collector, God the ogre. Why would a God like that become flesh? Who would stay for such a God as that?

But I fell in love with the God of the magic cave. Again a childish God? Yes, but a God who led me on; a God who could grow; a lovely, loving God. Caves are scary too, like dreams. But caves are not snivelling.

Thank you God for your benediction. And for the chance to be born close to the earth. Amen.

AIDS and
St Augustine

St Augustine was sexually promiscuous. Heterosexually, according to the evidence. Then he was converted. He became a bishop, one of the two or three greatest theologians of the Christian Church, and a saint.

Had AIDS been rampant in Carthage, his home town, Augustine was in the group at risk. His conversion may have come sooner, it may have been just as complete. It would have been, though, a deathbed conversion and we would have done without *The Confessions*, *The City of God*, and some of the insights of the Protestant reformers. The Catholic Church, the Protestants and the Orthodox would have been quite different. The non-Christian part of the world too. On the whole for the worse.

But Augustine didn't get AIDS. Venus he knew well. Venereal disease, fortunately, he did not.

Christianity is full of such examples: John of God, Mary Magadalene, Matthew Talbot, Thomas Beckett. People who played life fast and loose and lived long enough to repent of their sins. They went on to live great lives and have a lasting effect for the better on the world.

There have been millions of others. People who tried the latest craze. Absinthe, duelling, promiscuous sex, chewing tobacco, driving while drunk. And millions of them survived and lived good lives. To the greater glory of God.

All humans do foolish things. And evil things. But the young are carefree and often careless, sometimes just ignorant. So the sins of the young are often quick. They are spectacular and sometimes tragic.

The sins of the old are secret. When they are tragic it is someone else who dies young. Look at the ages on the headstones of war graves, Aborigines, and almost everyone in the third world. They are the victims of the sins of the old.

How would society cope, do you think, if AIDS was caught by liars, emotional blackmailers, the greedy, the crass, and the rankly ambitious? Who would be taken from our midst and buried in secret? What excuses would be made then?

There would be calls then for moral rebirth and I would support them. I support such calls now. Sex that is selfish, that destroys people and relationships; sex that exploits; sex used to sell soft drinks, cars, computers, religion—that is not what sex is for.

But the wrong use of sex is not the greatest sin. Nor is the wrong use of alcohol or other drugs, bad as that is. Despair is the greatest sin. A total denial of hope. That is a sin against the Holy Ghost. Despair says nothing can be done, God's love is powerless, Augustine can die in his sin for all I care because, when all is said and done he deserves to anyway. Despair denies the sinner the choice of conversion. Beside that sin the misuse of sex is a peccadillo.

So I am against despair. There is hope, I say. God

loves you no matter what. *Keep them alive so they can be converted* is on my banner. Keep them alive now. Because God loves all sinners, and because there are Magdalenes and Augustines out there and I can't wait for them to be converted.

Roebuck Charlie Winter

Roebuck Charlie Winter was the most selfish man I ever met. He's dead now and I wonder how he's coping. He was old when I met him and they reckoned he'd mellowed. He must have been a champion in his prime then.

Roebuck thought chiefly of himself. Once, during the war, he got some peanuts in the shell. It seems they were rare in those days. Well Roebuck took the bag of peanuts to the toilet and locked himself in. He sat there alone, read the graffiti and ate the peanuts. Of course he left the shells all over the floor for the cleaners, and the bag. That's how the story got out.

Roebuck's wife was pinched and wizened like grass too near a gum tree. Somehow it was known that Roebuck ate a large brown onion sandwich every night before bed. It was to tone up his muscles ... or was it his kidneys? I don't know. Mum always said that if you ate onions you'd have no friends but at least they could find you in the dark. Roebuck's wife looked pained from years of sleeping with onions.

He fancied himself as a cricketer. Actually he wasn't too bad. He had a good eye and thick arms and could belt the ball a bit. And once they made the mistake of letting him captain. Well he batted first and hogged the strike. Then he fielded where he'd get all the ball and bowled himself every alternate over. Once he hurt his back and asked for a poultice. 'I shouldn't laugh,' giggled litle Jackie Darmody every time he told the story for years after, 'but he made me do the poultice. I didn't mean to, but I burnt him. He had to go to hospital. Anyway it gave his missus a break from the onions.'

Roebuck loved fresh air. If you worked with him you froze if he got to the windows. Bang, bang, bang, he'd open them. He was a noisy man, old Roebuck, like his lawn mower. He was an early riser. Sunday morning at six, out there he'd go, engine roaring. Poor Dinny Henry, his neighbour. Actually Dinny says that once he got his come uppance on the early rising.

When Roebuck rose, everyone awoke. He turned the radio on loud. He rumbled. When he showered you could hear him down the street. He whooshed and whooped. Cold water! It kept him something or other, I've forgotten. Well, this day a cow got in his garden. Not that Roebuck grew much. He was a cutter, not a nurturer. But he whooped out of the shower, flung a towel around himself and burst out the door. 'Out, out, out', he shouted. The startled cow departed. But Roebuck's door slammed shut.

Mrs Roebuck would not be roused. She slept on. Dinny reckons that she shut the door. And she might have. I'd have shut the door and nailed it. And Roebuck tried the windows and the doors, one hand on the handle and the other on the towel. Dinny was at work at eight o'clock to tell everyone. Had he won the lottery he could not have been more excited. I don't know how Roebuck got in, but he got to work late. Nothing was said. But we had a great laugh.

God have mercy on Roebuck Charlie and on us. Help us be so secure in your love that we pay attention to others. Amen.

Rest in peace

Aunty Bid always said that she wanted to be buried in Boorowa. 'They have big funerals in Boorowa', she'd say. It was almost a motto for her old age and it seemed to give her comfort.

When she died, faithful to her request, we buried her at Boorowa. There were the priest, a couple of altar boys and seven of us. It was a struggle to find enough able-bodied men to carry the coffin. Aunty Bid was right about Boorowa funerals, it's just that the she hadn't lived at Boorowa. No one knew her there.

Anyway, it was a fair enough send off; hardly any people I admit, but the mass was nice and Father said something appropriate and if you have to be buried there are far worse cemeteries than Boorowa's. If you're a Catholic you won't want for familiar names on the headstones next to yours and in spingtime there are blue bells and daisies and Paterson's Curse in the paddocks round about and it looks beautiful. Even in the drought the country around there looks okay and there's something to be said for being part of it, something to show for your eighty-six years as it were.

Not like Arkwright's wife. It wasn't his fault. He was old too, and pretty near as doddery as she was, so when she died he had her cremated. Not that I'm entirely against cremation. I am a fair bit. Partly a strong Catholic memory, all the prohibitions of my childhood and youth. And partly feelings I have about the sacredness of graves and bodies.

You can think what you like about cremation as such. I'm not talking about that. Mrs Arkwright had more people there than Aunty Bid, and she had her name up on the board outside: '9.30 a.m. Mrs Arkwright'. At 9.25 they lined us up at the back door, at 9.30 the doors opened and in we went. There were a couple of readings, the priest said something about death and the resurrection (he didn't know Mrs Arkwright just as the priest at Boorowa didn't know Aunty Bid), then someone pressed something and the coffin was gone.

'Go out the front door please', the attendant said soberly, and out we went into the sunshine. We stood looking at the flowers and exchanging those kinds of words and actions you exchange after a funeral. Mr Arkwright kept repeating, 'Ten minutes. That's not much after eighty-five years. Ten minutes.'

And it is not.

I agree with Aunty Bid and the people at Boorowa. A funeral is worth a day at least. And a body's worth a headstone. Not a monument to the person's achievements; monuments pass. But headstones remind us that bodies are good but lives are better, and that life does not finish when our molecules are consigned to the ground. Cemeteries are holy places because in their way they celebrate life, and lives.

Thank you God for life. Teach us to value it and to celebrate it. Amen.

Homeless

Max and I went to the *Gracelands* concert. It was different from what I'd expected. Especially Ladysmith Black Mombazo. They kept singing, 'Homeless, homeless, moonlight sleeping on a midnight lake'.

What's this 'moonlight sleeping on a midnight lake?'

We decided we did not know, and the rest is in Zulu. But the memory of those men on stage dancing and singing, 'Homeless, homeless', that's what stays. Surely that is the message.

'Homeless.' Everyone is homeless a bit I reckon.

Our hearts are homeless, Lord, and never shall rest until they find their rest in you.

Homeless? That's when you don't have a home.

Home is your place.

It's where you rest.

Not just a house. People have been at home in a caravan or a cave. Some have been homeless in a castle. They have no place to rest. They are restless. They are wanderers; too active, disturbed, troubled. Restless is not free. Having a home is being free, it is a place to be free, a place to find yourself.

Home is having shelter.

Shelter is protection from harm; it is refuge, and safety. It is feeling at home. Some people feel at home more than others. They do not need a house. Before Europeans came to Australia Aborigines felt at home everywhere in this land. They did not need houses, being naturally at home.

The Europeans when they came were not at home. After two hundred years some of us are still not at home. We are homeless, we learnt nothing from the Aborigines about being at home in this land. Some of us are still wanderers, restless in Australia, disturbed and troubled. We have nowhere to feel free; nowhere that is our place.

'Homeless, homeless, moonlight sleeping on a midnight lake.' That's why the music touches me. *My heart is homeless and will never rest, Lord, until it finds its rest in you.* I am always a bit homeless even when I am most at home. That's just the way it is.

So I understand a bit what it is like to be homeless. So all those people without shelter are a part of me and my life. They are restless and I am too. Like the Jews of old, wandering in the desert. Wondering. Maybe it would be easier to go back, to cop out and stop struggling? Will I ever get anywhere? Maybe just pick a nice, cool oasis and bomb out? Just sit and exist?

Then I remember Ladysmith Black Mombazo dancing.

Once I told an African friend, 'I am going to learn to dance'. He looked stunned. 'Learn to dance? You do not need to *learn* to dance. In my town the moon is out, someone has a drum, we all dance.'

Sure we are all homeless, a bit. But we can dance. 'You are wanderers in the desert but you will be my very own', it says in Exodus. That is the reason to dance.

God of the Dance help us make our home in you. Be our shelter Most High. Teach us to dance. Amen.

In heaven already

I have written about Fowlhouse Dabrowski before. Fowlhouse came to a country town, with an unpronounceable Irish Christian name—given to him by a fiercely nationalistic Irish mother and an equally unfamiliar Polish surname—the gift of his father and a long line of European forebears. So someone christened him Fowlhouse and he was known by that unlikely epithet until he finished school and at old boys reunions ever after.

I mention him again now because Fowlhouse once told me his idea of hell. 'Hell', he confided as we sat waiting to bat, 'is fielding at cricket for ever.' I knew then what he meant and the feeling has never left me. Fowlhouse and I have this in common—a profound inability to play cricket, especially to field. Fielding is a constant fear and misery. In close it is the terror that a ball will come hurtling at me and I'll miss it, or worse, get hit. In the outer it is the boredom—the hours of counting grass and the slow descent into despond.

When I am fielding I can imagine hell. That is why, at least in a pharisaical way, I was good for so long. An eternity of that, I thought—no thanks, it's not worth it.

I suppose there are a lot of hells. Waiting for news when you know it will be for the worst; the terror of feeling that you don't exist; total and unutterable loneliness. What's yours?

Gary Catalano, the poet, says it is being in a place where it is too late to learn the meaning of your life. Too late, because you failed to reach out and touch 'the braille of the stars'. Blowing your chance, we used to say. One go and she blew it. Not by accident but by choosing to. By saying no to life either once, profoundly, like Lucifer, or time and again, slowly, so that you're dead and gone long, long before the doctor pronounces it. Like the man in Shirley Hazzard's *Transit of Venus*: 'He had long since become the views he had never contested: perjured acquiescence registered in an inward shrivelling of lip and chin'.

I used to be afraid of hell. Some people who taught me meant me to be frightened. I thought that somehow, suddenly, I would make a mistake and whoosh, I'd be gone. As if God were there, sword in hand, waiting for me to make a mistake. But now I'm not, for death changes nothing. *Now* is my chance, my one go. If I do not learn to enjoy God now, I never will. This is the time for me to run my 'light hand across the braille of the stars'.

Faust sold his soul, the story says, for wealth, knowledge and beauty. When the time came for him to die the devil didn't need to take him, Faust had been in hell for years. I want the opposite, to be alive all my life so that when death comes I will live forever. On the way to heaven we are already in heaven.

Creator God, recreate me all my life and forever. Amen.

All he learnt

McGilligutty's father loved 'In the Mood', the Glenn Miller version.

This was in the fifties before poor people could afford record players, so he heard it only when it was on the wireless. By the fifties Glenn Miller had been dead ten years and so his records were not played all that often. Nostalgia was not the thing then and ten-year-old records were just old fashioned or played in sessions like 'Memory Lane' on Saturday night.

So when 'In the Mood' came on the wireless all the kids and Mrs McGilligutty were shooshed and he'd stop and listen until it was over. Eventually he discovered that if you tuned the wireless to 2WG on Sundays around lunch time, The Coconut Grove, a local dance spot, had a music session that used 'In the Mood' as its theme song. Then he heard it, all or part, about three times in an hour.

Then the film arrived—*The Glenn Miller Story*—and he took them all to the pictures. He very seldom went to the pictures but that night they all went down to the Strand Theatre and saw it and cried at the end when Miller's plane crashed in the sea.

Why 'In the Mood' was so important no one was told. Maybe it reminded him of someone or some event. Maybe he and McGilligutty's mother shared a memory, though neither of them let on. Or he may have just liked it for itself.

He also liked 'Ring the Bell Watchman' and 'Souvenir' but he knew no great music. Bach, Mozart, Tchaikovsky even, were a mystery to him. He never attended a symphony concert in his seventy-five years. Old Man McGilligutty had no education. 'Everything I learnt', he'd say, 'I got from Sister Euphrasia at Pingilligo convent'. But, though the Old Man thought the world of Sister Euphrasia she hadn't taught him much. He'd learnt to pray from his father. Sister had taught him the mechanics of reading and basic arithmetic, but this learning had not opened the world to him. No one ever said to him, 'I really love A.E. Houseman. Here, take this book of his poems and try them.' The chance to listen to music, then, at Pingilligo, was minimal I know, but there were poems and novels about; but no one showed him.

Old Man McGilligutty and Sister Euphrasia are dead now. There is no point in apportioning blame. Probably Sister Euphrasia was uneducated too, even though a dab hand at teaching tables and reading.

McGilligutty's children also like 'In the Mood'. It reminds them of him and of listening to the wireless long ago in their half-dark kitchen. But it is not the kind of music that takes you beyond yourself. It is not poetry or art. Mozart's reputation is safe in the face of Glenn Miller. No one told McGilligutty's father that.

Creative God, send us teachers who know poetry and music, who point us beyond ourselves towards you. Amen.

A Christian Brothers Boy

McGilligutty was sick at breakfast. His mother said it was just nerves. Then he set off to walk the short distance across Dungog Street to the convent school. There he stood with all the other Last Year's Grade Two. Soon Brother Dailey came across the yard to collect them. They were beginning school at The Brothers. McGilligutty was about to become a Christian Brothers Boy. He was seven.

The Flats school was not one of the great Christian Brothers colleges. They wore the same tie as Westerley College but that was it. CBC, The Flats, was on the country circuit. The famous men, the Brothers of Renown, didn't get to The Flats except by accident; just occasionally one on the way up or the way down. In the annals of the Brothers The Flats was an oddity. Some of the city men were not even sure where it was.

But it shaped McGilligutty's life.

The Brothers' housekeeper was Miss Whistle. She'd been a barmaid with McGilligutty's mother and so

McGilligutty did messages for her. He, his brother and sister were often at the Brothers' house. Some of the Brothers were very human men, good to talk to or listen to. They had been to places McGilligutty had never heard of, like Gympie and Charters Towers. Some of them had a sense of fun. The good ones stood high in McGilligutty's regard. He was open to their influence.

Some he didn't like. One or two he detested. One or two were cruel or weak or odd in a way that repelled him. But he decided that they were the exception.

Anyway the Christian Brothers, good and bad, became 'learning' for him from seven until he was a man.

The Flats was not a great school. It was deficient. The Brothers there, the good ones, were tradesmen teachers. That is not to denigrate tradesmen, it is to say

that they were not well read in the classics, in literature, poetry, art or music. They had gone to the kind of school he was going to; they were not men of culture or wide learning but they worked to push boys through exams. McGilligutty regretted that later and still does, sometimes to the point of feeling angry. But like the parents and the son in McAuley's *Because*, he and his teachers were all 'closed in the same defeat'.

They were not closed in their regard for people. For this McGilligutty gave and still gives thanks. He learnt from them that good teachers care for their students. It was a theme throughout his schooling. The men he most liked were caring in an ordinary way. They taught him football or cricket, they stayed around to talk. He told his mother that they owned nothing, not even their watches. They witnessed camaraderie and he found it and them attractive.

'Tis a dignified business to make folks think', one of them said, quoting C.J. Dennis, another Christian Brothers Boy. Somehow they managed to make McGilligutty think. They managed, too, to touch in him the feeling that teaching was an honourable thing to do. Later they taught him how to teach.

And they witnessed to their belief that God is a part of every bit of life. Whether we win or not.

Wonderful counsellor, Mighty God, for the good and the bad, thank you. Amen.

Fights

Some families fought about cricket. Was Lindwall the greatest bowler or O'Reilly? Could they be compared anyway? Some families fought about families. They are the really serious fights. What Aunty Gladys did. Why Grandpa sold the farm. 'Keep out of family fights', my father always said. Our family fought about religion.

The fights were not about theology. They were about whether we'd say the rosary now or after the 'Jack Davy Show' on the radio. They were about whether father should say the extra bits or leave them out. They were about the time father broke into the litany with, 'Wake up all of you', and all of us, Mum included, said, 'Pray for us'.

Then there was serving mass. When there was a heavy frost and we'd been up late and bed seemed the only reasonable alternative, nothing, neither tears nor illness real or feigned, made any difference. If we were on to serve, we served. The reputation that we had for punctuality and reliability was entirely Mum's doing.

47

We fought for goals far more tarnished.

The night before confirmation there was a fight. Mum found three questions I didn't know the answers to. Three questions in the whole catechism! 'He won't ask those', I said. 'He might', she countered, 'and you have to know them. You may not get confirmed.' Poor Archbishop O'Brien. He'd have confirmed us anyway. He had to. At our school the lad from Tangmallang-malloo would have topped the class. Well I stayed up late, learning them, crying, pleading, acting faint to no avail. And I was woken early. I said them over and over. He asked me something easy, of course, and with everyone else I was confirmed.

Another fight was about processions. I hate religious processions. I did then and I do now. I have never been to a religious procession I liked. And we had regular processions. I loved the incense. I loved the candles and the colours, the flowers and the hymns, but not the processions. That they took up a Sunday afternoon made them immeasurably worse. We went very grudgingly. The nicer the day, the bigger the grudge. The only consolation was watching old Mrs Mintov, the Orthodox lady, standing in her garden making signs of the cross as we passed. I have never gone to a procession willingly.

Am I glad my parents won many of the fights? With reservations—I know what I dislike and why. I am not inclined to get trapped by nostalgia. I know some paths that lead nowhere and I found out early. And I learned a lot.

I grew up without good books, music or art. I found them later at teachers college, at university, from my friends when I left home. But I knew about good magic and myths, about flowers and incense and the sun shining through stained glass windows on brass in the afternoon. Before the sixties I knew a little about meditation and chanting. My childhood was steeped in ritual. It was lived close to the earth. When later I saw great actors I already knew about drama.

It is strange when I go back. It was not a beautiful church. The ceremonies were not well performed. The sermons I think were awful. But later when I was able to let go the fear, when I found out that the world did not stop at the horizon, I had a few grains to plant a crop with. Maybe the fights provided the fertiliser!

God some things are worth fighting for. Give us the grace to make a stand. Amen.

Increase my faith

Over the years I have developed some reflex actions. Like when the phone rings I say to my wife: 'You answer it'. And I have this prayer I say: 'Lord increase my faith'. I picked it up once when someone was trying to teach me to pray. I often catch myself saying it. It creeps up unawares. 'Lord increase my faith.' It sounds as though faith is a thing or a liquid! But no. I suppose I should say, 'Lord make me more faithful', but I know something of what I am asking and I trust God knows exactly. After all faith is God's gift in the first place.

Faith is easier to explain when you see a faithful person. I met a person of faith the other day.

Simon Farisani, a young black South African, became a Christian in 1963. He gave up the many gods of his tribe for the one God of the Christians. He began to work for the church. Not long after he and his white boss went to the zoo. His boss, pointing to the baboon, said, 'Simon, there is your cousin'. Simon thought he was joking. He pointed to the gorilla, lighter in colour. 'Boss there is your cousin.' He lost his job on the spot.

Simon stayed a Christian. Many white Christians told Simon that he was second class, inferior. Simon objected. He stood up for himself and his people. He was jailed three times. He was tortured by the guards. Electric shocks, beatings, isolation. His body could not cope. Three times he had heart attacks and he was in hospital for one hundred and six days.

'Do you still believe in your God?' a guard asked. 'Yes', he said. 'Yes.'

I met Simon at a church at Redfern. He sang and danced. 'I walk tall in the Lord', he sang.

Can you give someone faith? Well God can. And if someone asked me I'd say: 'Go looking. Find the people who are faithful and watch them. People like Simon, and Dorothy Day. Read those gospel bits on faith, or find a good worship community. I know they are hard to find but they are there. You must search!

In the town where I grew up they'd say, 'G'day. What do you know?' as a greeting. 'Not much', you'd reply. It showed a lot of wisdom that reply.

As I've got older I'd change it. 'Hardly anything', I'd reply. A few things. I know that God loves me and that I'm important. I know that God could cope without me but has chosen otherwise. I know that I am free or could be if I dared. Simon Farisani is freer than I am even when he's in jail.

I also know that I must keep searching. And I've become surer that faith is in reaching out and looking. Looking out to see like Thomas, the doubting one. 'Unless I see I will not believe.'

Thomas has had a bad press. He was neither foolish nor unfaithful. 'Those who have eyes to see let them see', Jesus declared. Thomas was taking him at his word. He was not looking inward. He was intent on seeing evidence for the resurrection, here and now.

Lots of searchers ask the same question. 'Show me that you believe', they say. 'If you believe that God loves you, how come you don't look loved? If you believe that God loves all persons, how come you aren't loving towards them all? If I see I will believe.'

Lord increase my faith. Amen.

God bearers

Ten thousand men are standing in a park listening to a speaker. 'Sisters,' the speaker says to them, 'we are all meant to be mothers of God. For God is always needing to be born'.

'How is God born?' they ask. 'What does the speaker mean?'

God is born poor, in a stable. God is given birth to by people who let God into their lives and then go out, unafraid. God is born to people whom the world rejects. 'There is no room for you in the inn.' God is born from those people.

'But we are men.'

And sisters too. And mothers as God is Mother.

'How can God be Mother? God is powerful and strong, like a volcano, like a man.'

'My father was not like a volcano', someone says.

God feeds us. God provides. God heals and nurtures, lifts me up to her face. God is a broody hen who will protect her chickens. Whenever you feel warmth, nurturing, comforting; whenever you cry, think of God-mothering.

'How can *I* give birth to God?' a man asks from the back.

'Listen', says the speaker. 'Listen to the world. Like an old woman. Become wise through living your life. Enjoy the beauty. Do not be ashamed to cry. Learn to hug and do not be too quick to give explanations. If someone says 'You are a real old woman' regard it as a gift.'

'And what about me?' a burly man says near the front.

Be powerful. Use power with honesty. Tell no lies. Know that you are beautiful and that God delights in you.

> *Behold you are fair, my love;*
> *Behold you are fair;*
> *You have doves' eyes.*

Be there for people. Wait. Men can be good at waiting, as a mother is. God waiting. Like the prodigal father and his prodigal son.

Be a person. Do not be pushed around and do not push. Persons are not things to be pushed or to be used.

Creator God, make us persons. Create us new all the time. Help us to create ourselves and others.

Know the stories of our people. Learn them from the elders of our tribe. See them in this land, taste them, smell them, get in touch with Creator God in this land.

Creator God, send your Son to calm and quieten us as the storm was calmed. Send him to stir us and send us out as he sent Mary Magdalene to say, 'He is risen. Rejoice.'

Spirit God, wisdom covering all the world like the love of a wise old woman, touch us.

May we dance and dance and dance with you here in the Spirit, Lord.

May we be mothers of Christ, carrying Christ in our hearts and bodies. May all people find Christ born in us. Amen

Doing and teaching

I admired Fintan Inkwell. I cannot remember if I liked
him. Liking did not seem an appropriate emotion at
the time. He was thirty-eight and called, quaintly, the
Master of Method when I was a trainee teacher and a
gauche eighteen-year-old down from the bush.

He was a very good teacher. He loved teaching.
'There are two kinds of pride', he said once. 'Filthy
pride. That will get you into hell. And professional
pride. Without that you will never be a good teacher'. I
don't know if anyone else thinks of him as quaint but
as I look back over the years I think it a useful description. He was odd in an interesting way.

'If in doubt, leave it out', he'd say; or 'If in doubt ...
throw it out'. I've often wished I could take his advice
on both more often. 'Press on regardless', was another
saying. He is the only sober man I have ever seen go
to sleep at the dinner table, his knife and fork in his
hands. He used to work extraordinary hours and his
body couldn't always keep up.

I can remember no idle chatter but he loved a good story. There was the Brother he knew who kept a jar of lollies on his desk to give to students who'd had some success at lessons. One boy, after getting all his spelling right, was duly called to the desk. 'What did you get?' his mate asked as he returned. 'One lousy jelly bean!'

Fintan was persistent. Some would have said stubborn. This trait he'd inherited from his father. Years ago there was a tram strike in Brisbane, where the old man lived. The tram men wanted better wages. The tram department sacked them all. So old Inkwell never rode on a tram again. He'd rather walk than give support to those he saw as unjust.

Fintan gave me the gift of valuing teaching, but not overvaluing it. 'A good teacher looks forward to the students arriving each day and is delighted when they go home at three-thirty.' He also told us, 'You'll know you are a good teacher when the students can do without you'.

In those days we gave observation lessons—a trainee teacher and a class with the rest of the trainees sitting at the back observing and noting. Things like how you asked questions, how well you listened, how well you had the class working.

My first observation lesson was a disaster, unmitigated. It was on 'The Praying Mantis'. Me, up the front rigid with fear, a class of forty-five grade fours, quite co-operative really, and all those people down the back. If the forty-five minutes before being hanged are any worse than I felt, then they are terrible.

But afterwards, after the criticism, Inkwell said, 'You will be a good teacher'. I believed him. It was a great gift he gave me; his confidence.

I seldom saw him after that. And he died suddenly, too young, before I thought to write. Maybe he knew and was pleased I could do without him.

Thank you Father for Fintan Inkwell who has become part of my story. Amen.

Once upon a time

Imagine the year is 2088. Don't try to picture the cars or the buildings. Isaac Asimov, Ursula Le Guin and countless others have done that already. Picture a person, someone your age. She has your surname, maybe, and looks just a little like you. This is your great great grandchild and she has become interested in the family history. This person is investigating birth certificates, marriage certificates, old photos, old school magazines. She wants to know what you were like because you are part of her story.

So she asks her grandmother. Her grandmother didn't ever meet you but her father told her stories. Things that you said or did. Some incidents remembered from your childhood, the photos of you that survived, the special memories and the trivial things that for no special reason someone passed on. Maybe they will have something you wrote or they will have some record of the things you thought important, the books you read, the people who influenced you.

Then you will be one of her ancestors, someone a trifle quaint. 'They used to wear funny clothes in those days' they will say of you. 'Imagine thinking things like that', they may say of your most treasured beliefs and thoughts.

But no matter what they find out they will never know the whole of your story, even if you write books or become famous and have books written about you. No one will know it all. Not even now when you are alive, here, can anyone know your whole story. You are too complex, too simple, too ordinary and too wonderful. There is just too much to know for one lifetime. That's why some people believe in heaven.

But one day, somewhere, perhaps a researcher will be reading the old papers, looking for some information and will notice the one mention of you, the day you won the sack race at St Maroun's school sports in 1979, and the researcher will wonder who you were. 'What was that person's story?'

What is this person's story? It began about 1972, or before. It will end God knows when. It is your chance, your go at life. Here, in this go, you can meet God because God is here for all of us. God is here, in Australia and everywhere and always has been. People have found God here for forty thousand years and for two hundred years, and they will keep doing it.

André Malraux, a French writer, said that the twenty-first century will be religious or not at all. You are part of the twenty-first century and of all centuries. Because you are here the world will never be quite the same. You are part of its story, part of my story, and it and I are part of yours.

Once upon a time there is you. And this story will be told, at least partly, by you. Who you become is partly your choice; who that person in 2088 becomes depends a little on you, too. I think that is exciting.

Creator God, you began our story and you are part of it from beginning to end to beginning. May all people, as they read my story, find you between the lines. Amen.

The old man

By the end they couldn't get him to wash and he sat there on the verandah of his crumbling presbytery and growled and looked over the town whose people he had loved and served, comforted, terrorised and ordered about for fifty years. And when he ate, much of the food stayed on the front of his cassock. 'Relics of ancient grease', Chipp the barber said. Chipp had a way with him and, even towards the end, could cut his hair and laugh and tell jokes and be oblivious to all the signs of decay. 'You'll be one of my pall bearers Chipp', the Old Man would say and then snort. 'One day soon.'

Well the day came and Chipp was a pall bearer and they closed the whole town. Except for Cress, the chemist. Cress was making some point or other but most people chose not to notice. Maybe he was a Mason. This was in the old days.

At the time Old Jimmy Moriarty was Young Jimmy Moriarty and he was MC for the diocese so everything was done properly. The Hibernian men wore their green collars. The Children of Mary wore their cloaks and veils and medals. The altar boys walked in twos wearing their white gloves and shoes instead of their red slippers because today they were walking outside. And slowly they led the procession after mass from the church, down the hill, across the bridge, around and up to the top of town then down Balowra Street back to the grave beside the church; this church that they had helped him build. And they buried him there under a great granite Irish cross. 'Benefactor to the Town' they put on his headstone.

Daisy Downes used to tell stories about him for years after. Daisy had come there on the staff of the Catholic school and she was a natural storyteller and the Old Man was a natural subject. Once he fought the tennis club. 'Catholic Tennis Club' was painted on the sign on the high fence until the old man decided that the new kindergarten needed to be built exactly where the court was. That fixed the tennis club.

He wasn't always like that. There was the time he came home without his boots, his socks in his pocket. He'd given the boots to a young husband out of work. He gave things away, his own and other people's, all the time. Once they collected money to give him a trip to Ireland. He took it down to Tregilles' Emporium with a list. 'All of these are to get a box of groceries at Christmas, Stan', he said. He wasn't going on a trip and they'd have to put up with him. Especially the Sisters in the sacristy. He gave them a hard time. Poor young Sister Ignatius!

He was an ecumenist before anyone heard the word. Once the local Protestant choir sang in his church for the mission; they'd written a mass for the occasion. He got into trouble for that from the bishop, but never mind. But if he felt he'd been hardly done by he was a hard man. There was this woman editing one of the

papers in town who libelled him. She agreed to settle out of court: a hundred pounds' worth of raffle tickets he decided. 'Which raffle?' Molony was asked as he was setting off to her office to close the deal. 'The one we drew last Saturday', he said. Rough justice in a frontier town on the edge of the Irish empire!

God our benefactor thank you for your gifts. Make us broad enough to rejoice in them as they come to us. Amen.

Marriage

'You know what used to really get me when I was a kid? Do you know? It was the way they used to talk at school about marriage. They used to talk about how married people should behave and about how great it was and there was I sitting thinking that it wasn't like that at our place. I used to feel awful. I'd think I must be strange or odd, because my parents weren't happy. There were always bloody fights. You know what I used to do? I used to kneel on the stairs outside and listen and pray. I'd say 'Please stop them fighting. I'll hold my arms up if only you'll stop them. I'll be good, I promise, just stop them fighting.' Sometimes I'd go to sleep there. I hated them fighting. They only got married because of me. Mum was pregnant. She won't talk about it though. Never. I found out myself, later. They'd never celebrate their wedding. I still don't know the date. As if it matters. I couldn't care if they were pregnant. I think that was the trouble. They just never told the truth. And she's been ashamed. For all those years.'

'I suppose you won't get married yourself', I said when he paused. He was really steamed up.

He changed though. 'Oh yes. I am married. It's the best thing I've ever done. Going on ten years this August. But that's different altogether.'

'Different?' I asked, interested. He seemed so much calmer.

'Yeah. I suppose I've been lucky. Or blessed; a gift I suppose. I've thought about it a lot; why we like being married and why our kids seem to like us being married. Different from my parents. I still think it would have been better for everyone if they'd split up years ago.

'One thing is the *truth*. When we met we got to know each other a bit, we used to talk and talk.'

'Yes I can imagine', I smiled, but he didn't take any notice.

'Then I got shifted. I got sent up to the bush for a year for my work. You know what we did? We wrote letters and we sent tapes. We've still got them all, though I haven't read them for years. They might make a book. Maybe not. They're probably embarassing. Anyway writing letters and sending tapes gave us the chance to say a lot of things, to work things out so we knew where we stood; a bit anyway. You never finish finding out really.

'And we decided we wouldn't be forced to do anything. We were going to get married if we wanted to, not because it was expected or anything. We broke a few of the rules. I remember we drove ourselves to the church when we got married and I insisted that Clair made a speech and we didn't have a cake. Aunty Rita was very annoyed but I told her, 'It's our wedding Rita'.'

'I reckon you wouldn't have any fights then?' I asked as he paused for breath.

'No fights. Arguments and discussions though. Someone taught us that. Said that part of being married is learning how to argue properly. Not being hurtful, telling the truth, two equal people and *listening*. That's the big one, being able to listen. And change. I've had to change a lot you know. Especially I've had to learn to listen.'

'You said blessed back there.'

'Yes. There's a fair bit of luck and I believe that I've been blessed. God's been good. I mean God is good but I feel especially that God's given us a lot. Especially friends. Clair's my best friend, you know. I think that's one of the absolute rules. You'd be crazy to marry someone who wasn't a good friend. My parents aren't good friends even now.'

Thank you God for people who can learn from life. Teach us to listen, to give and to change. Teach us, too, that there is always hope. Amen.

Ties that unbind

Hercules O'Shea always wore a necktie. I've seen him ploughing with a tie on. First walking along behind a horse and plough and then as he became more affluent, driving an old blue Fordson Major that he'd bought second hand. 'I'd feel naked without it', he'd say if you'd remark on his tie. Most men at The Flats saved their ties for funerals, weddings, court appearances and for the more formal Holy Name Sundays. O'Shea thought that his predeliction for neckties, even when he was ploughing, probably came from his Tralee ancestors. He'd never been there to see, but his father had always worn a tie and he'd heard reports that his great-grandfather had. 'Maybe its genetic', he'd say, 'or maybe it is a sort of localised race memory. Some long dead O'Shea who survived some dreadful experience because of his tie. It might be natural selection'.

Hercules' eccentricities were not limited to his neck apparel. His name also set him apart. That was his father's idea. Just at the time Hercules was due to be born his father had gone to a family funeral at Frogmore. It was a long ride in the sulky and it was one of those pleasant sunny days in early October when for a change the whole country is green. So Old O'Shea was in a reverie by the time he got there and as he stood beside the grave and they recited the five glorious mysteries of the holy rosary, his eye wandered over the nearby headstones. The one nearest him was that of his aunty, Florence Mary O'Shea. Next to that was her son Hercules. So he decided that if that was a boy his wife was carrying, its name would be Hercules. It had a ring to it, Hercules O'Shea, and he liked bells.

A few weeks later Old O'Shea and his wife and son were in the baptistry at St Mary's church. 'What is the child's name?', the priest asked. 'Hercules?' he thundered when he heard. 'That's not a saint's name. It's a pagan god's.' Old O'Shea was undeterred. 'Hercules Patrick then', he said. So the Father said Hercules very softly and Patrick very loudly as he poured the water and Hercules went out into the world with the local church frowning over his name but without a care in the world.

That early experience of convention flouted may have been the source and strength of his later eccentricity. Whatever the cause, undue influence of peer pressure was never a problem for Hercules O'Shea. Not that he sought to be different. Standing out caused him quite a lot of pain. 'Hercules—what kind of a name is that?' his teacher said. But for some reason he just went ahead. 'What do you mean?' he asked in response to an insincere 'Are there any questions?' Being honest himself, he presumed it in others. 'Don't be afraid to ask', they'd say, so he would. 'You're not allowed to ask that question', was the offended reply. But Hercules O'Shea just carried on. Ask and you shall receive. And if sometimes a rebuff was what he received, never mind. There's no question you can't ask; we have nothing to fear from the truth.

Unpredictable God, thank you for the gift of eccentrics, questioners of all conventions. Teach us to dare to question. Amen.

Moose

Moose could not teach two cats. We all agreed on that. He couldn't teach anything. In spite of this inability Moose spent his whole adult life, save five years at the end when he retired, as a teacher. When I first knew him he was principal of my school, a woebegone school, but a school nevertheless.

Moose taught me Latin. Or that's what the timetable said. Latin classes consisted of Moose up the front teaching third and fourth grade, eight- and nine-year-olds, and Berrigan and me down the back. Berrigan was doing Latin because he wanted to be a priest. I was doing it because I had won a bursary and doing a language was a condition of my keeping it. I was thirteen.

The year before I had entered secondary school keen to learn Latin, geography, history, anything; but instead I'd encountered Sealey. Sealey was a wild, unpleasant man with a grizzled, grey crew cut and a temper. He was a reject from Westerley College and the other great city colleges, a man who worked the country circuit and who was passed on from school to school. He lived on the memory of an international footballer he'd coached at Bananatown in 1935. Sealey punched and yelled and bullied and Latin became unattainable. So next year two of us survived in the Latin class with no vocabulary, no grammar and, alas, no love of the subject. And Moose.

Well, I did not like Moose but his staff loved him. I knew that then and I have heard it from some of them since. They admired him, too, because in a time and church when adults were often treated as children, Moose treated adults as if they were grown up. In fact he demanded that adults be grown up.

Moose trusted people and he had an inbuilt detector of sham. He had a free-ranging (then I thought it sometimes cruel) wit. Childish adults caught it full on. The precious or the pretentious went down in flames. And he resisted bullies.

Once, then, I did admire him. It was the day Mrs Bumper took him on. Mrs Bumper looked like Big Chief Little Wolf, a famous wrestler of the day. Her son, Thug, later became a standover man. At this time he was a standover boy and somehow he had fallen foul of Moose. In the manner of those days, Moose had hit him and Thug had complained to Mother. Mrs Bumper came across the school yard (school had just finished) in a cloud of dust and ire. She called Moose out onto the verandah and told him to put his fists up and be prepared to be belted.

'Mrs Bumper,' he said politely, 'I am tired and hot. You are tired and hot and angry. Now go home and have a cup of tea. I'm going to do the same. Then you come back and we'll fight.' He turned and walked into the house. She went home and stayed there, probably bumping Thug to ease her pent-up anger.

It has taken me years to appreciate Moose. I wanted

to learn Latin and he could not teach me. He was in the wrong place for me. But he was in the right place for his staff. No one is good at everything. He was an adult educator before his time, so some of him was wasted. I give thanks with mixed feelings. *Amen.*

Horrible's end

I have been to hundreds of funerals. Country funerals when I was a child when hundreds of people would be there. City funerals too. Once a tiny funeral with just the priest, the funeral director's men and me.

Country funerals were big events. Some of the people came great distances. At Catholic funerals the family would meet the night before, at the funeral parlour, and say the rosary. Or the people would come early before the funeral. 'Hail Mary full of grace', one side would call out. 'Holy Mary ...' the other side would answer, sometimes before the first side had finished.

People came who were not Catholics of course. Some would wait outside the church, others would go in but they'd sit quietly at the back. Catholics would do the same when there was a funeral at another church. In some towns the priest would say, 'You cannot go into other churches even for funerals'. But people did. 'You have to give people a decent send off', they'd say.

Sometimes the funeral would be very sad. Like the time Micky Slavin was shot. He and Murdoch had wagged school and gone hunting rabbits and the gun had gone off accidentally. We were about fourteen or fifteen and we all felt miserable standing there watching his coffin carried out of the church. Now and then funerals were joyful occasions, almost. A local identity who had grown old graciously and people gathered to

say farewell and to tell yarns. Like old Rose Collins. She always had a way of saying things just so, and at someone's funeral years before was heard to whisper very loudly, 'There won't be no snow flakes where Horrible's gone!' Even Horrible had a big funeral, though; a last gift from the people and a hope that when they in turn were the ones being carried out people would be there for them, to pray, to set them on their journey, to rejoice in what was delightful in the person, to forgive what was not.

And so I still go to funerals if I can. Not that I like death. I don't. I am scared of dying and I deeply miss friends and relations who have died. But death, like birth, is a very big event and it needs marking. That's why I don't like some modern funerals. Crematoriums are an example. You have half an hour. Quick. In. A few words. Push the button. Gone. Out. Half an hour to celebrate a life! I want them to spend at least a day sending me off. And I want a lot of music. 'Now Thank We All Our God' and the Magnificat and 'Glory to Thee, Lord God!' And I want a jazz band playing 'I get a kick out of you'. I want people to read poetry and tell stories. And I want flowers; corn flowers and yellow daisies and daphne if it's out, and waratahs and wattle—piles of wattle—and poppies or petunias. Masses of them.

Bede Jarrett said somewhere, 'Those who die in grace go no further than God and God is very near'. I believe that and I think it is worth celebrating.

Creator God, your son Jesus died. Then he rose from the dead. Now dawn and flowers and music have new meaning. Thank you. Amen.

Jesus Christ!

'Jesus Christ!', he said. He had dropped a four-pound hammer on his foot and was leaping around. 'Jesus Christ! Jesus Christ!'

Behind him, standing quietly, was an old grey man, tattered at the edges, raising his hat. Each time the exclaimer said Jesus Christ, Old Grey raised his hat.

He is making a prayer of the exclamations. Or maybe Old Grey *is* Jesus. Maybe he's acknowledging his name. 'Jesus Christ', the man yells out and Jesus doffs his hat.

I've met Jesus, you know. Often.

She was sitting up the back of my Year 10 class all one year. She didn't speak to me despite my efforts. The occasional grunt was all the reply I received. I often felt like throwing things at her or yelling. She did not respond to my jokes. My best-prepared lessons touched her not at all. 'Jesus', I used to think. Sometimes she smiled at me.

Another time I met him at a railway station. 'Can I

have a dollar for a coffee mate?' he asked. 'Coffee,' I thought, 'he doesn't want coffee'. I gave him a dollar and he didn't say thanks. He went off towards the exit. 'See you in heaven', I thought. 'See you, Jesus Christ.'

Like a John Ogburn painting. The world is redeemed. He is everywhere. There are resurrections of flowers and trees in those paintings. There are, as Les Murray says, absolutely ordinary rainbows. Plain old ordinary resurrections.

Because Jesus Christ is risen from the dead I am an absolutely ordinary rainbow, and you are too. Jesus Christ is in the absolutely ordinary.

And the word was made flesh and took up his dwelling amongst us. I have heard him. He says choose. He says jump. He says take a bloody risk mate. I stand on the edge. Sometimes, just occasionally, I jump and the stream carries me.

Once I thought if only I'd been alive in Jesus' time. His first time I mean. Now it's Jesus Standard Time. Jesus Summer Time, too. But I mean when he was walking around in Galilee. Then, I used to think, it would be easy to decide. No church to get in the way, no books, no people. Just plain, clear choice.

Have you ever made a big choice? There are no big plain clear choices. It was just as hard then, sisters and brothers. It was just as hard to decide then.

There were people then in Galilee, in Judea and Samaria who saw him, bumped into him, and didn't see him at all. Is this the Christ or are we waiting for another? And while they tarried he was gone.

So here's your choice. There's a poster that says, 'You may be the only book on Jesus Christ that some people ever read'. You may be their absolutely ordinary rainbow. (Excuse me, Les, for knocking your phrase around like this, it is such a brilliant phrase.)

Parent God, you sent your son for us. Help us to meet him everywhere we go. Amen.

A kind of loving

Praying is a kind of loving.

Praying is talking to God in a familiar way—calling God by name. Father, as Jesus did. Mother. Talking to my brother and my sister. God.

Praying is inviting God to be part of my life. Come in, sit down, be part of me. Be me. Everything I do, I do for you. And for me because you are part of my life. You *are* my life.

I praise your name. I love your name, my father, my mother. God. Just as I like my own name. It is all for you, to say that without you all is nothing. Welcome to my life.

Here. Just as it is. Be part of my world. The part of me I like. The parts I don't like. Help me to want myself, to love myself as you love me. All of me. Help me to want what you want, to live with myself. What you want is not often easy to know. There's no easy way of finding out. Sometimes I just have to do things and hope. Be the reason for my hope, Sister God.

Loving is about groups. Come and be part of our group. Share yourself with us, Father God. Teach us to share you. That we may become lovers. Great lovers. Help us to love. May we be a society of friends. A society of lovers. May we change the world with you, Brother God.

Praying is a kind of loving. It has to be *learnt*. Loving is not just the sudden flash. The Ah! That is just the start. Or not the start. We all feel Ah! hundreds of times. Ah! isn't he beautiful. Ah! isn't she delightful. Ah! the sea at dawn. That's the *in love* bit.

My father gave me one piece of advice. 'Never give advice', he said, and I hardly ever do. But here's one piece of advice. If you fall in love there's nothing more certain. You will fall *out*.

And that's when loving can take over.

That's how you make friends. With God as with anyone else.

Loving is learnt by heart. James McAuley said that. Loving *is* learnt by the Ah! sort of feeling. Sure. But loving comes from doing.

But not overdoing. Practice does make perfect. But only if you practise the right thing. Gently, one thing at a time. Even on a bad day.

A champion is a person who plays well when she's playing badly. Martina Navratalova said that, about tennis. It's true about love.

Father, give us what we need. As you do all the time. Everything is a gift. I am a gift. A *surprising* gift. *I'd* have designed me differently. Thanks for the way I am. Sometimes I find that hard to say. On the days I'm playing badly.

Forgive me. Teach me to forgive myself. The things I do wrong. The sins. And help me to forgive the others. So that I can love them. Sister God. Mother. And so they can love me. In the silence and in the noise. Where I like being. Where I don't. Be there with me.

81

And keep me from evil. Not bad things. That's different. There will be bad things. That's life. Help me to live, accept and love those, but never to give in. But evil. Help me avoid evil. Doing evil, being evil.

Come God, Father, Mother. Be part of my life. Let's be friends. In good times. In bad times. Be my brother. Be sisterly to me. I need you. Amen.

Why are we here?

'We're here because we're here, because we're here, because we're here.'

We used to sing that on train trips and bus rides when I was a teenager. It went on and on with no finish. That was over thirty years ago and the Second World War was not long over. I think our fathers may have sung it going off to war and they taught it to us.

One day last year I sang a bit of it to a group I was working with. 'Maybe that's it', a woman said to me afterwards. 'Maybe it is enough just to be sure we are here.'

It is enough for some people but not for others. We're here. So what? Why are we here?

I'll tell you a story. It is a true story.

Eli Wiesel is a Jew who was arrested while still a boy and sent to the Nazi death camps. There, one day, he was forced with all the other inmates to watch an execution. Three people, two men and a boy, were to be hanged. All the prisoners were to stand at attention and watch.

The victims were brought out, stood on stools, and nooses were placed around their necks. The stools were kicked away. The two men died instantly, but the boy was too light. Very slowly he choked.

As he hung there struggling a voice from the crowd called out, 'Where is God now?' Someone replied, 'God is there at the end of that rope'.

That comment is very good theology. We can never go anywhere God has not been.

'I don't know why I am here,' that unnamed prisoner called out, 'but I know that God is here too. God is at the end and is carrying us to the end.' That is part of what incarnation means. God is made flesh amongst us, making what seems to have no meaning full of meaning.

We just need to see. We need to be open to what is revealed. That is what artists do especially. They learn to see or to hear. It may be just rocks, deserts, skies to us. Artists see relationships. That is why artists are so important—painters, composers, writers, storytellers. They are sources of revelation for us.

Revelation is the collection of intelligible events that can make our lives intelligible.

Artists say two things. They tell us the stories about our past that tell us some of the truth about our present and maybe our future. And they give us the courage to take our own present and future seriously. If artists care so much as to see and hear these things, maybe it is worthwhile us seeing and hearing as well.

Lord that I may see, that I may hear. You have given me this chance to experience things, help me to experience them to the full. I don't want to miss out on any of it.

So we're here because ... a million things. But we're here. Let us make the very most of it.

God, here with me, hand in hand, teach me to see and to hear. Amen.

Just a working God

I do not believe in reincarnation. Lots of good people do—the Buddhists and the Hindus for instance. They believe that people keep coming back. But I don't believe them. One go, that's what I believe in. I get one go and that's it. When I'm gone then I've had my go.

So what I do now had better be good. It's the only chance I get.

I do not believe in Roxy Cola. Because they don't believe in me. Do you know what they think up there at Roxy Cola? They think that I am a thing. A consumer. The same as everyone else. I consume therefore I exist. When I die that's one less consumer. Well they're wrong about that.

I am unique—the only me there is. And, after a long time working on it, I like who I am, mostly.

I do believe in incarnation.

Incarnation means God had a go too. Once. Once upon a time Creator God sent Son God to have his one go. And that go made all the difference in the world. Jesus is God's great gift to the world.

So are you and so am I.

You are a work of magnificence.

You are a treasure. And you are called to do the work of God. Make the very most of your go at life.

Put *your* face here...

Treasure... work of God.

Because you are very rare. You are a single sunset. God dancing in the world. You are a poem. A sheer delight. You are a song. God is singing. Now. Not getting ready. All the way to heaven is heaven. Not for later. But now.

My life is God's gift to me. God's work. What I do with my life is my work. My gift to God. It can be a beautiful gift. A beautiful life. Whatever it is like. Whatever I am called to be.

How do I know? Listen. Be quiet.

God gives you hints. The things you are good at and the things you are not. The things you want to be. Sometimes accidents. Or they seem like accidents. God is a very subtle god. A push here. A prod there. Little signals. And big. Sometimes you'll think you have it worked out. Then bang. Whoosh. Or whimper. And you're off on a different way.

Courage. You are called to be as game as Ned Kelly. As game as Caroline Chisholm. Follow the leader. God. Thy kingdom come on earth. As it is in heaven. Sometimes dreary but always, always alive.

I want to say on my eighty-fifth birthday, 'I wonder what I'll do with the rest of my life'.

Father you are there, part of my one go at life. You are calling me. Most of all you listen to me. Help me to listen. Teach me to hear. And give me courage. Amen.

Trees

There is no shade in Murgatown because there are no trees. They cut them down, one by one or by the streetful.

The currajongs went to widen Bullock Street. And anyway they were ruining the gutters. The palm trees went in Boycott Road. They were a haven for starlings and starlings have lice. The pepper trees in Merton Street smelt and children got sap on themselves and came home dirty. Pepper tree sap is hard to remove so they removed the pepper trees. And the red gums in Lumley Lane, they stayed but they had to be cut back. Just in case a branch fell. Someone could remember someone's grandfather being killed by a branch. The world is safer without branches. Now the red gums are mutilated. They give no shade.

There are no flowers in Murgatown. Flowers need water and water is scarce. Once Mantis Hogarth grew flowers. He carted the water in two buckets on a pole. But they criticised. What a waste of water! Better used for the poor. Better used for something else. 'Fancy Boy', they said. So Hogarth's flowers withered.

The sun glares down on Murgatown. The youths race up and down in Bullock Street. It is wide with no obstruction. The gutters are straight. The shops are straight. They are painted white. Dust settles on them. And the youths race up and down. In Boycott Road no old men sit. They used to. Under the palm trees and talk. They sat under the Tree of Wisdom and swapped yarns and memories. Of course there are no starlings. In Merton Street the children play on the road or do not play. As they no longer climb the pepper trees they come home clean. As they do not climb the pepper trees they do not see over the fences and the houses either, so do not know that out there there is a world bigger even than Merton Street. At least they are clean. And no one has been killed by a branch in Lumley Lane. Nor has anyone seen the white cockatoos that used to nest there and their screeches do not fill the air as they glide and dip, great flashes of white and yellow against the sky. Lumley Lane is a dull lane but it is a safe lane. Life is in the safe lane in Murgatown.

I hope that I shall never see Murgatown without a tree. May they plant and plant and plant. So that old people may sit in the shade and tell the stories of the past. So that Mantis Hogarth may grow flowers—shade flowers and sun flowers. May there be pepper trees and dirty knees. It is not good for people, especially someone's grandfather, to be killed by a falling branch but let there be branches; for people to climb out on; for people to swing from; for galahs to nest on, and cockatoos and magpies. And may the currajongs lift the gutters. Who wants straight streets or white shops all in a row?

God, you walked in the garden in the cool of the evening. May we not fear to walk in your garden. May we not fear the trees. Amen.

Call me
unpredictable

There's a Laurel and Hardy film, I don't remember its name, in which the pair fall foul of a gangster. He threatens that should he ever meet them again he will skin them alive. He does meet them and the film ends with our two heroes, looking miserable as only they can, Ollie blaming Stan as usual, with heads and hats intact but skeletons from the neck down.

I saw the film when I was five or six and for days I was overcome with sadness. It seemed such an unfair and terrible thing to happen to these incompetent but funny men.

At five I was some kind of fundamentalist. The metaphor passed me by and I was stuck with the literal meaning.

It is appropriate at six to be a fundamentalist, though even then I blushed with shame one day when my brother said to Enormous George McAuley, 'The chairs at your house must be made of cement.' I knew that some truths were safest left unstated or dealt with by using what I much later learnt were euphemisms. I must admit that neither then nor now could I think of a euphemism to describe Enormous George. The chairs at his house must have been made of cement.

It is not appropriate for adults to be fundamentalists. Fundamentalists rob metaphors of their meaning. They make life a miserable shade of grey. What is far, far worse, they make God a miserable shade of grey. They make God tiny. They pare God down to fit into their own tiny, limited minds and experience. They deny people the magnificent unpredictability of God.

When I was six I was not really a fundamentalist. It's just that I was into concrete reality. Planes flying overhead were taking souls to heaven. How else would they get there? Films were real because I saw things happening and I believed my eyes. But I knew God was a mystery because no one I knew tried to make God small. 'Why did God do that?' I asked when Grandma died. 'She's gone to heaven. I don't know. Just pray for her', summed up the replies. They were not great theologians, my parents, but they were honest. 'I don't know' is one of the great theological answers, when followed quickly by 'But how great God is, and loving'.

My parents were not poets either. They knew some verse. 'The old man walked to the sliprails', Mum would begin. Sometimes Father, to annoy me, used to say a bit of doggerel he'd learnt at school, 'You're a fine little fellow said he, tapping me on the head...' But they had some feeling for the poetry and the unpredictability of life. There was no chapter and verse that explained everything. Nuance was a word that was seldom used at our place but its meaning was part of our lives. Don't ever make the mistake of thinking that you know the completeness of God or that you know exactly what God wants. That's fundamental. But it's not fundamentalist.

Unpredictable God, may I live in joy in my uncertainty. Amen.

A very big God

Fawzi, Chaim and I have this in common, that Abraham is our father. Fawzi is a Moslem. His religion goes back to Abraham. Mohammed is, Fawzi says, the greatest of the prophets. Chaim is a Jew. His religion goes back to Abraham. The Jews gave the Christians the Bible. I am a Christian. My religion goes back to Abraham. Pope John Paul says that the Jews are our big sisters and brothers in religion. To understand myself I need to know my Jewish family, my big sisters and brothers. Jesus is God. My religion comes from him. Jesus was a Jew right up until the day he died. And rose.

Fiona, Stephen and I have this in common: that Jesus is our salvation. We are all Christians and say together the Lord's Prayer, 'Our Father who art in heaven...', just as Jesus taught us. Fiona is an Anglican. Steve is Uniting Church. As Protestants they share in the tradition which gave Christians back the Bible, which taught us that God is present in everyone's experience, that convinced western Europe that slavery is evil. I am a Catholic. I accept the pope as my leader in religion. I am part of the tradition that gave us the mystics like Teresa of Avila and Therese Martin and that gave us Chartres Cathedral. As a Catholic I like sharing something valuable with Pope John XXIII and Dorothy Day. As a Christian I am glad to share much with Bishop Desmond Tutu and Fiona and Steve and the other Protestants I love and pray with.

Arvind, Huong and I have this in common: that we each find that religion is the best way to make our lives work. Arvind is a Hindu. He has millions of gods. He has taught me how to meditate and be quiet in the presence of God. He has taught me how to make more of my Catholic way of praying. And he has taught me

some great stories that I use in my prayer and my teaching. Huong is a Buddhist. She has no god, in a way. I do not really grasp what she means. Huong is a searcher. She is following a path. She has become a very good person and I like and admire her.

'Allah Kabir,' Fawzi says to me, 'God is big'. God is infinite, my old Catholic theology reminds me. There is much that can be said about God. Otherwise heaven will be very, very boring. There is an infinite God to love, adore, praise—and describe.

Religion loves, adores, praises—and describes God. It can never finish. God cannot be captured. Of course some things that are said are wrong. If I say something's black and you say it's white then one of us is wrong. We have contradicted each other. But if I say God is one and you say God is three, who is wrong? No one, says Athanasius. That's what Trinity is all about. 'Trinity', says Erin my wife, reading over my shoulder, 'is the teaching which most clearly says that God can't be captured'. If all that is said and prayed, praised and adored by all the Buddhists, Hindus, Moslems, Jews and Christians that ever lived was added up and multiplied by ten, that's not God. So there!

I said some things are wrong. If you say God is boring you're wrong. A lot of people act as if God is boring. They're wrong. If you say God is arbitrary, you're wrong. If you say God loves white people more than black people or men more than women or vice versa, you're wrong. And if you say that humans can capture and gift-wrap God you're not only wrong, you are an idolator. God told Moses, our Jewish brother, 'I am who I am'. That's why it takes so many religions to worship, praise, love, and not even then describe God.

Meanwhile I'm glad I'm a Catholic Christian because I cherish the truths that God became a human and comes to me in the Bible, the community and the sacraments.

Thank you God that I am a Catholic Christian and thank you God for Fawzi, Chaim, Fiona, Stephen, Arvind and Huong, and most especially for yourself. Amen.

Play it again Samantha!

I met her at the Now Open, a quiet little coffee place at the corner of Walk and Don't Walk. She was a little the worse for wear. She had been drinking coffee all night and long into the day. Flat white with short black chasers. Her voice was crystal clear, with an edge, like someone wide, wide awake. 'What do you do for a living?' she asked. 'I teach', I said. 'Religion.' I knew that was dangerous. Admitting a professional interest in religion has a startling effect on some people. 'I was a Catholic once', they'll say. Or they'll tell you the most intimate details of their search for fulfilment, love or meaning. Religion brings out the best in some and the worst in others. She looked like one of the latter and my surmise was not wrong.

'I hate God,' she said, 'and I hate Catholics. By the way, what are you drinking?' I ordered a cappuccino and sat mixing the chocolate into the froth. She went on. 'It's a long story. It wasn't always like that. I made my first communion. I was six and it was at St Mary's parish! I loved that day. I talked to God, and Jesus and to the Blessed Virgin. Bah!' she exclaimed. She called for another coffee. 'I don't take sugar', she said. 'I gave it up for lent in 1961. I was sixteen.'

'You lasted till sixteen then,' I ventured, 'with God, I mean'.

'Oh, I lasted longer than that. It was my twenties. University, then a lot of reading and thinking. I just got sick of being ordered around by men. Sick of not being nourished. Sick of being expected to be an everlasting child. So I got out.' I ordered a pineapple donut. 'No', she said. 'They're fattening. Besides all the coffee has killed my tastebuds. Why do you stay? You look intelligent enough. And midly normal. What's the church offering you?'

'That', I said, 'is a good question. I stay because I feel at home, though it is often a lonely home. I read a lot. That keeps me going. I have been researching my roots, my Jewish roots first. Then, every now and then I hear someone or see something that feeds me. Like this. 'If it's good news for the poor it's the gospel. Otherwise it is not.' That sets me thinking and hoping. I suppose for me it's all based on my hope that the world is essentially good and I'm part of it and God loves me. I have a poster on my wall, it says *It's our church*. That's it, really. I believe it's our church. How you see the church is the thing. It's not a club or a team or an army. It's a group of sinful people, like the Last Supper. Some have been weak and some will be, but Jesus gives himself to them nevertheless. It's our church. The Jews say, 'The bashful cannot learn'. I've tried to give up being timid or easily embarrassed. I also work against being bullied. There are some people who think they are God's gift to truth and light; standing on the Rock of Peter, they say. Well lots of people have stood on rocks before, only to find they were standing on a hippopotamus.'

Standing on a rock

I'd finished my cappuccino. Samantha grinned. She rose and walked out into the air.

Can God cope?

I nearly didn't make it.

It was like this. One night when he was about twenty, my father, Bill his brother and a friend of theirs were going home in the sulky from a dance. It had been raining and when they got to the creek on the Balowra Road the water was up so high they didn't dare cross. So they turned upstream until a place where it should be shallow and set off to cross. It wasn't shallow. The horse just disappeared. The sulky sank. Bill and my father went back to the edge. Their mate found himself closer to the other side and swam there. In the dark he made his way to Chubbs'. They wouldn't let him in but let him sleep wet on the verandah. So much for charity. Father, as he later became, and Bill walked soaking back to Bendick. In the morning they found the sulky unharmed and the horse drowned. A good horse, too. 'Lucky we hadn't had a drink all night, otherwise we'd be dead.' There were all sorts of versions of the story but that one's official.

If my father, not then my father, had drowned that night I wouldn't be here. Would God have coped?

One of the German mystics (Yes Matilda he was a good Catholic!) said, 'Without me the universe cannot exist. Without me the least worm would surely shrivel.' I have thought a lot about that and am not sure of all its meaning, but he is on to the profundity of human existence. Because I am, I am inextricably linked with all that is. But what if I wasn't? There's surely something to learn from that.

Oh, I know you can say, 'Well you are and you didn't have a choice'. They could add that I should live as if I might die tonight and work as if I would live forever.

But what if I wasn't?

Mavis Doherty finds it hard to believe that God can cope. Her problem shows itself in a myriad of ways. She takes responsibility for the world. 'Show the visitors to the door', she tells her husband Rufus as he bites his lip and shows the visitors out. 'Don't forget your cardigan,' she tells her daughter Maud, 'and take the zinc cream for your nose'. The day the Bishop came to the school to say the St Malachy's Day mass she told him how to tie his cincture. 'He'll need two chalices', she told the acolyte. He judged that one was enough. What if Mavis Doherty's father had drowned?

God can cope.

And I am here for better and for worse. I am part of the universe but I needn't have been and there are several thousand million people around in roughly the same position. And God can cope. And strangely, so can most of the people. Maybe it comes from being made in the likeness and image of God.

For some reason that God knows best, people often cope.

We all live in tension. Between coping and not. But it's strange how many people interfere with other

people coping.
'Do you want another cup of tea?'
'No thanks.'
'Sure?'
'Yes, I'm sure.'
'Go on, have another cup of tea.'

Thank you God for coping and for trusting us to cope. Help us to trust others. Amen.

If he could see me now

Les married early and it did not work. He went and talked to the priest. 'You made your bed, Les. You'll have to lie on it.'

When Les met Irene it seemed it would work. She was a Catholic, too, though her family had not been good Catholics and she'd never been much part of the faith. She'd gone to a convent school for a while but it all touched her lightly.

They found a minister—a kind old chap—who married them, and they settled down. They got on well together. Les went to mass often. He sat at the back and felt like a leper. Sometimes he took up the plate if he was asked. Les also said some prayers, especially at night.

Les was frightened. He was scared of God. He was terrified of dying. He remembered the retreats. He remembered the day when they had all pushed their bikes down the hill from the retreat house after Bombadini's talks, for fear they'd fall off and die, or get run over. Bombadini knew, it seemed, hundreds of people who had died trying to cheat on God. People who'd said they'd go to confession next week and died this week. All kinds of deaths. Falling off roofs, under trains, out of bed. One after the other they'd tried to extend their pleasures. One by one God had got them. And they'd gone to hell. Bombadini was sure and Les believed him.

Now Les was fifty-two and he felt sick. He went to the doctor and was told that it was too late. 'I'm sorry, son,' the doctor said, 'you won't last six months'.

Les saw the priest. A different one from long ago. He went to confession and the marriage was fixed up. I don't know the details. Les sat down on his verandah to die. He prayed and prayed and feared death.

Mick Mordley was a retired alcoholic. Ten years retired from work and thirty retired from alcohol. He had known the highs and lows and at seventy-five was still searching. He spent his time reading and listening, watching, talking and visiting. He saw Les sitting on his verandah.

Mick called in a lot at Les's. He'd talk to Irene about this and that, then sit for a long time on the verandah with Les. 'I am terrified of dying', Les told him eventually. And he told him about Bombadini and how they'd pushed their bikes for fear of being killed on the way home. 'I used to think that I'd never do anything wrong because with my luck I'd get run over before I got to confession. I've been to confession, Mick, and I'm still terrified.'

'Bloody hell, Les, you're wrong', said Mick.

'Bloody hell, Mick,' said Les, 'or bloody heaven, that's what I'm afraid of.'

'Les, it's your inheritance. You have to go and say 'Here I am Lord. I'm your son. I've come for my inheritance.' Mick looked earnest. 'He made you Les, he loves you. He finds you delightful. He always has.

When you were struggling and hurt. When you and Irene made a go of it. When you sat like a leper up the back of the church. Now he wants you to look forward to your inheritance.'

Well Les changed. The pain was horrible. Yet Les became calm and beautiful in a way. 'I am going for my inheritance,' he'd say. 'You know, Mick, I wish I'd believed that always. If only Bombadini could see me now.'

And Les went to claim his inheritance.

God, Mother and Father, you have adopted us because you love us. Give us the confidence to walk in hope as your children. Amen.

Saturday drunks

Drunks on Saturday mornings go off the hotel spruce, hat cockily on the side of the head. They have a determined look in their eye. 'I am just going down the town. I'll be back in a little while', they say. You know they won't. You know it will be a long time. But there's nothing you can do so you nod. You are part of the pretence.

Drunks on Saturday night come walking across the street. Normal. They must look normal. If they come lurching, swaying from side to side, they are not drunk. Then you feel relieved. If they act, they are sober. A determination to be normal means they are drunk. They will be maudlin or sick. They will be sorry, for themselves and for everyone. There will be a fight or she will go off in a huff. She will feel aggrieved. She won't sleep in the double bed but will sleep with one of the kids instead. Probably the eldest, because she thinks he understands and he is on her side. And he too will be miserable.

Sometimes drunks on Saturday nights bring home an accomplice so she can't be angry; or a lobster which she likes but will not eat. 'I won't be bought', she says. Sometimes they are really late and she will fret. She will ring the police. 'Have there been any accidents?' Sometimes she threatens: 'I will leave and take the kids.' But she doesn't.

Sunday they will go again. 'Hair of the dog', she says. If the pubs are shut for Sunday someone is serving beer out the back or there's the club. Maybe they'll be late. Drunks on Sundays look sorry for themselves.

Drunks on Saturday are not real drunks. I mean they can stop. They can come home drunk and lie on the floor in the hall and think. 'I will shoot myself or stop drinking'. And just stop. Saturday drunks are bored or lonely. They have no art. No one taught them poetry. They have nothing to do. Sometimes they live in the withering wind of criticism and interference that cuts everything to size. Or the close horizon of limiting expectations. Saturday drunks live in towns and cities where there is no shade. They live in the glare.

Saturday drunks do not know what they are good at. They live in football towns. Or towns with tough hands. Or towns where there is no conversation. Saturday drunks live in towns with their mates but they have no friends. Their wives are not their friends. No one has taught them how to grow. They live in a world of much talk but no talking to. They are the wasted generation.

Alcohol is not the problem for Saturday drunks. Alcohol is like bread. It is necessary for eucharist. Like people, wine and bread are needed to celebrate. The Saturday drunk knows that. But they are not enough. And it is not enough to know the difference between right and wrong or to pretend to know. Pretending to know is worse than not knowing at all. And the

Saturday drunk knows that, too. But cannot easily say it.

Saturday drunks need art. They need to create themselves. With help. They need broad horizons. Saturday drunks need shade, not the withering wind of other people's fears and their own. Saturday drunks are tall poppies but nothing grows in fear. Poppies are nothing when chopped, they have no shapely bush. They need no cutting back. Pruning is not a good metaphor for Saturday drunks.

Compassionate God, forgive the Saturday drunks. Send them teachers who know poetry and art. Send them friends. Flood them with your compassion. Amen.

A sacred place

I do not like the plains, like my father before me. 'I don't like flat country', he'd say. I feel at home in the rolling country where there are granite tors on the rises and now and then a creek in the shallow, winding valleys. I love the surprise of coming over a hill, say there near Galong from the Harden side. I am touched by roads and tracks that wander in and out between the trees.

When my father was young there was no made road between the family farm and town. There were just tracks. Once, coming home at night with some of his friends, sky larking, he reached out of the car and grabbed a possum from a low branch and pulled it in. The possum was not amused. Scratched, and angry with my father, the travellers went homewards leaving the possum to regain its tree.

When I travel along those roads and tracks I am filled with stories and I wonder how they felt, those Wiradjuri people who almost forever trod that country on the hunt for food, or on the way to corroborees, or later being hunted themselves, or being dispossessed. And I wonder how my people felt, the first time they journeyed there and all the times later. When they saw the paddocks purple with Paterson's Curse, or white with frost, or black after a fire. They are buried there now. Some of the places I know, and some of the stories. My mother's uncles, Hugh and Robert, aged nine and seven, drowned in Crowther Creek in 1867. They went to get the cows and the creek came up too fast. Their father found them next day in each other's arms, snagged in the branches of a tree. He went grey soon after, the story goes, and his health went.

A SACRED PLACE...

Most I do not know. The blacks' burial places are not marked and no one has told me their stories. All their God-discoveries died with the people; those people who trod my country and loved it as I do. And some of the whites' places are not marked. The poor ones, those who could not buy Gaelic crosses for their graves or windows in churches to ask prayerful remembrance for their souls. So things that made them laugh or cry or shun or desire have passed away or passed into the land.

But I imagine them. 'Pray for me', Great-grandfather John says in granite on his grave. I can read that, it's in my language. Pray with me they all say in the frost and the Paterson's Curse and the clear blue days and the dust that rises over newly-ploughed paddocks. The symbol gives rise to the thought. The signs they've left me lift me. And I go back again and again because that is where I am created and it teaches me how to create. These are my sacred places. This is where I was called into being. This is my symbol place.

Once I stood in the valley of Elah. 'If David killed Goliath, this is where he did it', our guide said. 'These are the stones, that is the stream.' I know exactly what he meant. God was in action here.

> *The pastures of the wilderness drip,*
> *the hills gird themselves with joy,*
> *the paddocks clothe themselves with flocks,*
> *the valleys deck themselves with grain,*
> *they shout and sing together for joy.*

My God—discoveries began and are rooted there. Alleluia.

Monopole Maloney

Ron, Fod and I were swapping yarns and Ron told me this story. I thought that you might like it too.

Monopole Maloney was not a church-going man, despite the suggestion in his surname that there had been Catholics back there somewhere. Monopole was described by the locals as the kind of bloke who lives on his wits. He did a bit of this and a bit of that. Had he lived in a seaside town you might have said import–export. In a town where people's fortunes rose and fell, or in some cases seemed permanently fallen, Maloney usually seemed to be at the worst successful and usually prosperous. Whether he was or not, he always managed to look prosperous, hence the name Monopole. Day and night, whenever he appeared in public a cigar stuck out of his mouth, sometimes lit and at other times not. It gave him a distinctive look in a roll-your-own town, sometimes even distinguished.

Well Monopole died. I can't remember if he was old. In those days anyone who was an adult seemed old to me. Anyway he had adult children so I suppose he was getting on. And when they read his will they got a surprise. Monopole wanted to be cremated. Not only that, he'd specified the crematorium. It was in a big city that was in those days of steam trains and unreliable country roads a long journey from where Monopole had lived and held court. It was a place where, for all his fame in the bush, Monopole was quite unknown.

On the day of the funeral they arrived at the crematorium, Monopole beyond all caring and his family and friends having travelled all night in dog-box carriages, red eyed from lack of sleep, cigarette smoke and the ash that used to fly in the windows of steam trains, a point often forgotten by romanticists today. There at the crematorium door was the minister who, in a few minutes, was to deliver the eulogy for Monopole Maloney, a man of whom he had just heard and of whom he knew nothing.

'Tell me something about your father, Mr Maloney', said the minister. 'What were the things that gave his life meaning?' The younger Maloney was stumped, and halfway down the wicket at that. What could he say of Monopole Maloney that would form the basis of a panegyric? 'Well,' he proffered, 'he liked the horses'. So the minister took as his text Matthew 6:26, 'Look at the birds of the air...', and said that people who loved nature were close to God. He mentioned St Francis of Assisi and pointed out other allusions in the scriptures to animals: lions lying down with lambs, good shepherds and two sparrows sold for a farthing. Monopole's friends, churchgoers and not, were highly amused and pondered on what the great man himself would think of all this. They supposed he'd probably laugh—hat pushed back on his head, Monopole sticking out of his mouth—while with stubby fingers he tried to calculate the odds.

Creator God, you watch over the lilies of the field and the birds of the sky, watch over us, fit us all into your wonderful plan. Amen.

Josie's grave

The road there comes along the spur, out of the orchards, and goes down into the valley. The cemetery starts at the road and goes away down the hill. The Church of England section is tidy. It has a lych gate and tall pines that moan in the wind. Its graves, near the gate, are old and expensive. The Catholic section has a large, gaudy, metal sign and a clutch of priests in simple graves; their headstones face away from the road and look over their flock below them.

Josie's grave is two-thirds of the way down the hill, way over on the left. The hallowed ground, then, stopped halfway down so she was well outside it. It was a sign, the priest said. He'd say the Mass for her early, quietly and without letting on. He'd take the funeral too, though he forbade that it be advertised. Only Pat and all those crying kids and the undertakers and her sister were to come. But he would not bury her in hallowed ground.

She had gone down to Sydney. She told Pat that her

sister was sick and that she wanted to see her. She had caught the night train; first the twenty miles to Railwaytown, with half an hour's wait on that windy platform, then sitting up all night in the dog-box. Now and then a speck of ash in the eye, all the time the discomfort. Marie met her at Central when the train stopped there at six thirty and they went to her house at Redfern. 'I've arranged it', her sister said, 'for this afternoon'.

There was no good asking Pat. He couldn't make decisions. She hadn't even told him she was pregnant. And there was no good asking the priest; she knew what he'd say. But Josie had had it. There were nine already and Helen, the eldest, was just thirteen. It was July and cold; Pat did his best but there was never enough. The thought of another pregnancy, another baby, more work, just crushed her. So she'd written to Marie and posted the letter quietly. She'd just have to take her chances. And then she'd just have to cope. And hope it didn't happen again. The thought of it depressed her. 'She must be really worried about Marie', Pat had thought and tried to jolly her up. 'I hope Marie's all right', he'd said as he put her on the train.

She was away three days and Pat met her at the station. There was a frost; he'd jumped up and down as he waited. She looked wretched when he saw her. Not just from cold or sitting up all night. He couldn't tell what it was but he knew it was very bad. Whack Kearins had his sulky there and he took them straight up to the hospital. Sister Immaculata saw her at the door. 'Whack, go down now and get Dr Galway. Bring him in the sulky. Tell him I said it's urgent.' 'Wait out here, Pat', the Sister told him. 'Sit by the fireplace. Get warm. I'll get the nurse to bring a cup of tea.' She went in and sat near Josie. 'How long were you pregnant, Josie?' she asked.

'Four weeks, maybe six. I couldn't have another one Sister. I couldn't. Am I dying?'

The nun was fingering the large rosary on her belt. 'You've got blood poisoning. It's very bad. I think I should get the priest.'

Josie lay there. 'Get the monsignor', she said, 'if you can. Will you tell Pat?'

She lived two days more. Helen stood there beside Pat, watching her die. She stood beside him at the funeral too. It was cold and raining.

The cemetery has long since passed Josie's grave and the new priest blessed the ground, unaware of her story, or aware. 'It's a sign', he might have thought.

Holy Mary, pray for us now and at the hour of our death. Amen.

Poor

When Uncle Joe Drover won the Silver Circle he gave
Kilrust's mother half. They'd agreed that if either won
they'd share it. Five pounds he gave her and though it
was mid-morning Sunday and the shops were shut she
went down to McGovern's butchers and found Ted
McGovern out the back mending something and he
went into the cooler and sold her a leg of lamb.
Dinner had to be late because it took an hour and a
half to cook.

Kilrust, thinking back, knew they often had to go
without. He remembered his father sewing wheatbags
together when they were short of blankets. He remembered that they never went on holidays. His first real
holiday at the sea was when he was nineteen. And
their house, always neat and cared for, was tiny. Hot
in summer, freezing in winter. He thought that the
things they suffered from—boils, chilblains and other
things—were probably dietary. Aunty Irene had had
rickets. At least their generation escaped that. Looking

back, Kilrust realised he'd been one of the rural poor.

Then he hadn't realised. After all there were many who were worse. There were the cherry pickers. When they came he was afraid of them. Not that they did anything to him. Occasionally they'd fight among themselves. The law said they could not drink alcohol but they did. On Saturdays when there was no picking they sat in the park near the railway station. He remembered they had loaves of bread, and wine. Their clothes looked untidy. They were poorer than he was.

And there were the Whitlows. They lived in the old house out near the saleyards. There were lots of children and Mr Whitlow drank. 'He was such a fine man when I married him', Poppy Whitlow once said to Kilrust's mother. Kilrust had gone up to their place once to play. The Whitlows didn't have a fridge or even an ice chest and Mrs Whitlow had given him a glass of luke-warm milk. It had been boiled so it would keep. And she'd opened a tin of peas, mashed them and made sandwiches. Even then Kilrust felt like crying because the Whitlows seemed so poor. He hated milk anyway, as some country people do. You can't trust milk where there are no fridges, and many country people drink black tea. But he drank the luke-warm milk and ate the pea sandwiches. He felt patronising and then guilty.

'Weep for the poor', thought Kilrust later. Poverty is bad for people. 'Smoking stunts your growth', said the sign in Coles Picture Book Arcade. Kilrust used to laugh at that when he looked at all his big friends smoking. 'Poverty stunts your growth', he thought. It robs people of art and music. It makes them satisfied with the mediocre. He had a picture in his head of poor Glynnis Whitlow, the eldest, one day in town. She was overweight and had bad teeth but was buying ten shillings' worth of cream cakes for herself. She took them to the park and ate them one by one. There was cream on her face and icing sugar on her nose and dress. To her ten shillings' worth of cream cakes was heaven. Poverty shortens your grasp. Poverty shrivels your soul.

Poverty is the least romantic thing in the world. It is not God's will. Chesterton knew that: 'I do not want to pull queens from their thrones and sit them on chairs. I want to sit all people on thrones'. That's easy to make fun of, but it's close to the truth. Heaven is not ten shillings' worth of cream buns.

Just God, stir us that we will not tolerate anything that kills the spirit. Amen.

You shall be as gods

Worried Arthur of Mullyan Siding retired and went to live at his daughter's at Bunjil Bunjil, and there he died. He left in his will that he was to be buried at Mullyan Siding but that the mass was to be at Bunjil. And he willed that the funeral procession, in those days a horse-drawn hearse followed by sulkies, was to go at walking pace from the church to the cemetery. Worried knew that that would take them four hours.

Well, Worried Arthur died in July and the day of the funeral was one of those miserable days you can get in those parts in July. It was wet, with snow falling but not touching the ground, and by the time the procession came around O'Connor's Hill and the cemetery was in sight the mourners were to a person stiff, cold, miserable and angry. 'Well Perce,' said Sniffy McInerney to his mate as they rounded the hill, 'there won't be any snow or frost where Worried Arthur's gone, anyway'.

It is a sign of Worried's effectiveness that sixty years

after, the story of his funeral is remembered, at least by me. Worried achieved some sort of immortality. That he caused only four hours of misery in his attempt is bad enough, but little compared with some immortality seekers. What of Hitler and Stalin? Think of the millions who suffered for their immortality.

But we all do it. Spread right across Australia there are headstones, foundation stones, cornerstones and millstones, put there or blessed or carved by someone hopeful that his then eminence, talent or notoreity would be remebered. Sometimes it's her eminence but more often it's the men. Women were more inclined to seek immortality in their children, tending to live not in their own generation but later, hoping to be remem-

bered as the little mother who slaved her fingers to the bone or gave up her chance for her children. Then there are the discoverers. Have you ever heard the account of the first person to see that Dame Hortense was going to be a great singer or that little Spotty Grimthorpe was clearly going to be the next Bradman? Like America, most famous people have many people claiming the title of Discoverer, all hoping that the comet will drag them after it and that they too will be immortalised.

It is becoming harder, though. Foundation stones don't last any more. They are bulldozed and a freeway with someone else's name covers them. Families are smaller. There will be no more little Irish mothers, because mothering now takes less than a third of a woman's life and the fraction is shrinking as their lives get longer. Andy Warhol pointed out that everyone can be famous for five minutes. But what about immortality? What about me? Will I be remembered?

The feeling is more frantic. The means are becoming often more vulgar, more violent, more evil. With television, a mad man or mad woman taking a gun to the population in Littletown USA can be seen live in Littletown NSW. How's that for immortality? Worried Arthur was an amateur by comparison.

I have a head full of trivia. I can't help it. I have a good memory. I know where I was when I heard that Marilyn Monroe died and I remember the year. I know all sorts of useless things. I try to forget some though. I make an effort to forget the names of assassins; I resist glory seekers.

I try to live in the present. 'What is the good thing now?' is my question. I do not always do the good thing and as frequently I do not know what the good thing is, but I've begun thinking that the painters before the Renaissance who didn't sign their work were onto something. The work was important, not the worker.

We used to write AMDG on our books at school. All my deeds for God, it means. I am beginning to see the truth of it. What is the good thing now? What would give God glory? If St Polycarp's church is for God's glory why put anyone else's name on it? I am someone's father but I have to live my life now while I have the time to do what I am called to. Christians do not believe in reincarnation. I won't be back.

God our Creator, help me live for the now. Help me to seek your glory, not my own. Forgive me the things I do that are just aimed at being above the crowd. In Jesus' name. Amen.

Whoopee! What a God

The Calathumpians build their churches without windows. If they could they would build them without doors. The walls and doors are painted beige. Nothing must distract the people from God. God is a mystery, beyond beyond. Calathumpians hate distractions. Windows fill with skies, clouds, birds, flowers, people, sheep, advertising hoardings, aeroplanes and floral curtains sometimes. They are, therefore, un-Godly.

The Calathumpians believe everything literally. Doubt is a distraction. And that's not all. So are interpretations, asking, thinking, confusion, mystery, metaphor, tradition and delight. Calathumpians hate metaphors because metaphors invite excitement. Metaphors are tense. They say 'It is and it is not' and that is a distraction; that is the most delicious distraction there is.

Excuse me, you Calathumpians, I am becoming enthusiastic.

I am not a Calathumpian!

The opposite of Calathumpian is Relisher. Another word is Sacramental.

Relishers built Chartres Cathedral and the Sydney Opera House, Notre Dame and the lookouts at Esperance and Echo Point and Bulli Pass. Relishers love skies, clouds, birds, flowers, aeroplanes and sheep because things distract them towards God.

Whoopee What a God!

Here are some Relishers: Chesterton, Hildegarde, Aquinas, Mechtilde, Cézanne, Gerard Manly Hopkins, Julian of Norwich and Henri Matisse. 'Do you believe in God?' someone asked Matisse. 'Yes, when I am painting.'

Chesterton was a great saint in the Relisher church. 'Bread and wine are important', he said once. 'Without them you can't have eucharist.' Chesterton loved things.

That's what sacrament means. Things. Water, wine, oil, bread, clothes, candles, salt, lights, glass, colours and smells and sounds. And feet, hands, heads, breasts, knees, genitals, ankles and elbows. If you can't stand things you can't be sacramental. Things distract us to God.

And another thing. Metaphor. If you can't cope with metaphors you can't be sacramental. This is bread and it is not bread. This is my blood. Take and drink. The time Jesus said this (you'll find it in John 6) there were Calathumpians around. 'Who can believe this?' they said. Fundamentalists all, Yuk! Blood. Erk! Bodies. It is no wonder they crucified Jesus. He kept talking about body and blood and spit. He even rubbed spit on someone's eyes. Quick, get the Dettol, we might get AIDS.

'Who made the world?' we used to chant. God made the world. Why? So we could find God in it. In water, bread, clouds, wine, oil, body and blood. And spit.

Whoopee! What a God. Amen.

Welcome to Australia!

White cockatoos remind me of God. They squawk and squeal and can walk on one foot. Galahs remind me of God. They are pink like the dawn. When God made the first galah he said, 'That was good. I'll do it again'. And he did, millions of times.

'Draw Australia? Draw a straight line', says Ogburn. He's a painter. 'God in Australia is a vast blue and pale gold and red-brown landscape', says Les Murray. He's a poet. God is in that straight line stretching out and out. God is in that pale gold and red-brown. And the cockatoos laugh with the galahs. What a God to make this fabulous place!

This is my place. Accidentally. Katie Prendergast, my great-grandmother, nearly went to America but she came here. So I write this in Australia. This is where God is and has been for ever. This is my time—1944 to forevermore. Now I can find God here.

God has been here a very long time. In the Dreaming, at Uluru, Mumbullah, Wilpena Pound. God reveals himself and herself to people and always has done. Sometimes the people look. Sometimes they do not and God creeps up or rushes on them unawares. Thou mastering me God.

You have to laugh—and cry—in this land. You would be a fool to think that we control this land. There are fires and floods. There are droughts. Coal mines explode. Here the land is in charge, and the air and the sea.

Welcome to Australia Pope John Paul. Discover God in a new way.

You need a sense of humour. So God made the galahs and the cockatoos.

In Australia God's votaries wear tattered shorts. They wear jacky howes and shapeless dresses and wide hats to keep the sun off. They talk to God in the vast blue and pale gold and red-brown landscape. They are not fashionable. This is not a fashionable country. It is too far, too hot, too dry. This is the great south land surrounded by sea, cut off. But not cut off from God. And the people laugh at themselves. We celebrate survival. We celebrate distance and quiet. We celebrate cities and newness. And our very great age.

So, welcome migrants and travellers. We are all travellers here in this, nearly the last of all the lands. But God has been here for a long time. Help us to discover God. Discover God yourself in a brand new, ever ancient way. Look at the rocks and the sea and the distance. Talk to the galahs. Try on some tattered shorts and a hat and walk and walk and walk. Outback. Dreaming. Inback too. Follow the streets and the roads, look at the houses, talk to this odd race with a sense of humour. Laugh with us. We have the cross in our sky.

Son God, shine on us. Creator God, creep up on us or rush on us unawares, the rush that never ends. Amen.

I'm sorry Robert

I think I named Robert Mugabe. It cost me two and sixpence and it happened one Lent when Sister Saline arrived in class with these small cardboard containers. She said they were Mickey Mite boxes. I presume that was the spelling. Maybe it was a Might box as in 'Always hopeful'!

Now Sister Saline said that if we filled our mite boxes with money and brought them back to school the money would be sent to Africa. Africa at that time was full of black babies—pagans who were just lining up waiting to be baptised. To be baptised they needed money; ours. In return for the money we got to name the babies.

Sister Saline was very convincing. As God's personal representative in grade one at St Joseph's school her word had credibility.

So my baby was called Robert. At the time I was not very imaginative. I had just lately completed kinder-garten in a class of ninety-three. Kinder had consisted

That's not a Catholic name...

of keeping quiet, sitting in long rows in a little room, hearing stories about how venial sins made white spots on our souls and every now and then asking to go to the toilet. Going to the toilet meant first getting Sister Vitas' attention. Then, permission having been gained, getting the whole long row to stand so that you could get by in an effort to make the door. By the time I got to the door the journey was no longer necessary.

My friends have been known to comment on my humility. I developed it in kindergarten! Some of my more adventurous classmates developed aggression, but not me. I chose humility. Ah! the good old days.

My choice of Robert, like my humility, was the result of experience. Carmody was first in line. 'What do you want to call your baby?' Sister Saline asked. 'Buck Rogers', he said. That sounded a fine name to all of us, but Sister Saline demurred. 'That's not a saint's name', she said. So Carmody had to settle for Anthony; with an aitch, the Catholic spelling. There would be no Antonys here. Wendy Wheatley asked for Adelaide, after her grandmother. That met the same response but Sister agreed that Mary might be added and the name was written down. There was then a list of Bernadettes, Thereses, Pauls, Dominics, a Philomena and a few Annes, and I chose Robert. I knew it was a saint's name because there was a Sister Robert at the hospital. I had thought for a time it was a girl's name because the only person I knew who had it was a nun. But in grade one my best friend was Robert McPhee and Robert Mugabe is named after him. I was an adult before I learned that Anselm, Declan, Aloysius and Stanislaus were also boys.

Well, times have changed and I'd like to say I'm sorry Robert. Let's let bygones by bygones. If you'd rather be called Todd, Buck or Stanley, feel free to change. Even if it's not a saint's name.
Your friend, Pius.

Alzheimer's ward

In St John's ward, *Bonanza* is on and Hoss and Little Joe ride across a Ponderosa that is too red because the colour is wrongly set. The old men do not notice.

I am sitting holding Father's hand. Today there is no response. Some days there is a flicker. Once he bent and kissed my hand. Another day, before his last sentences went, he asked, 'You're one of the Englishes arent you? He had long since ceased to recognise Mum, but when she died he missed her coming. She, too, used to sit and hold his hand.

The Major across the room sits at attention. He still looks dignified. The red collar on his dressing gown and the piping on the sleeves remind me of the officers' mess, but the dullness of his eyes suggests that he is not reminded. Who knows what memories, what joys and hurts are there. No one can know. To this secret place there is no password.

Charles has lost his dignity and his peace. He roars and bangs his bandaged hands on the tray locked across the chair to hold him in.

I thank God that Father, all but lost to us, is gentle still. I hold his hand. The nurses are busy. 'Hello Major', 'Hello there Jim, good today eh?' And I thank God that they treat my father with dignity and with compassion.

I often feel like crying in St John's ward. I often feel like shouting, 'Why is my father—gentle, humorous, intelligent—reduced to this?' Mum used to feel so hurt, so helpless. 'She died of a broken heart', Sister says. Maybe Sister's right: 'One day soon she will come for him'.

> *Clean wounds, but terrible,*
> *Are those made with the Cross.*

Maybe. This is not a clean wound. It has jagged edges and it throbs.

Alzheimer's disease is in the news. One night it was on *60 Minutes*, before Mum died. She rang and told us. I rang later but she could not talk. 'It's so true,' she said next time, 'they just go'. The long, long goodbye. They just slowly, slowly go.

People are nice about it, 'They have no worries', some say. I'd rather have worries. 'They do not suffer.' I think I'd rather suffer—maybe not. I am not a good sufferer.

The people who help me most are the ones who don't explain. 'I am sorry', they say. 'Remember when we used to dance, Perce?' 'I liked your father. He was a gentleman. I am sorry.' I can cope with that. Then I know what I miss. Then I can live with the grief that I left some things unsaid.

One day she will come for him. I believe that. I believe in resurrection, I believe that all this has meaning. Now it is in a glass, darkly, but I believe. One day I won't have to believe.

Now I hold his hand. Maybe tomorrow there will be a response, a flicker. Maybe he will kiss my hand.

137

Father, one day we will see together. Help me to hold on to that. Amen.